Seeing is
Believing

Signed
1st Ed

Believing Is
Seeing

By Parveen Smith

Dedicated To…

My dear sister, Sukvinder who is with the Angels

Order this book online at www.trafford.com
or email orders@trafford.com

Most Trafford titles are also available at major online book retailers.

Print information available on the last page.

ISBN: 978-1-4251-2196-9 (sc)
ISBN: 978-1-4669-7794-5 (e)

Trafford rev. 10/18/2018

 www.trafford.com

North America & international
toll-free: 1 888 232 4444 (USA & Canada)
fax: 812 355 4082

Seeing is Believing
Believing is Seeing

Contents

Acknowledgements

✡ ✡ ✡

First of all I would like to thank my husband Daren for his patience as I have been busy for the four months of writing this book. My children too have understood that this venture has been just like doing their own homework.
My special thanks go to Tristen, Tony, Moyra, Dean, Wei Ling, Karen and Paul for all their help.

Seeing Is Believing
Believing Is Seeing

Introduction

Have you ever wondered if there is anything out there other than us human beings?

Well let me tell you that there is. In my life I have used the phrase, 'Seeing is believing' or 'When I see it, I'll believe it.'

Now, at the age of 36, I have seen many things which are beyond anything I could have ever imagined.

I am very fortunate at this time of my life to be experiencing the things that are happening to me. I feel like the happiest person alive. My spirits have never been so high.

I experience guidance and assistance on a daily basis. I feel love and support around me all the time in a spiritual and physical sense, for I sincerely believe that I am in contact with Angels. It is my belief that they are there to help us in dangerous situations, for protection, to bring love or even to help us through sad times and illness. I believe, through my own experiences that signs can be left from angels, such as feathers, coins and visions of angel wings. These are relevant reminders of their contact.

I have also learned on my spiritual journey that 3 is a sacred number. It is The Trinity to Divine Truth. I regularly see the number 3 around me. Often, when I have glanced at the digital clock it is there. Any other number that also is divisible by 3 gives me messages too. I now understand the importance of this number as it also guides me.

It took some time for me to realise that I was on a spiritual journey after hearing thudding noises; things being moved mysteriously in the house: the electrical messages such as the television flickering when certain words were spoken were relevant reminders to my situation at that time: sightings of Ascended Masters and sightings of animal spirits.

Seeing is Believing

My life has changed dramatically over the last six months with the help of the Angels. Therefore, I would like to share these happenings with you.

Before you read on I shall briefly explain about Ascended Masters, Guardian Angels, Auras, Crystals, Oracle Cards, Angelic Reiki, Chakras and Past Life Healing.

The Ascended Masters such as Jesus Christ, Saint Germain and Djwal Khul were people who once were in the physical body like us. After their long commitment, dedication and devotion to their life mission on earth, these enlightened ones ascended to the heavenly realms. They may appear to us, to assist us with living in peace, truth and gain enlightenment.

Guardian Angels are with us from the minute we are born, they are with us to reassure and comfort us in our time of need. Sometimes they may appear just to let us know they are there. They offer us guidance in our lives whether we wish to accept it or not. These angels can appear as both male and female. Sometimes they are seen as twinkling lights.

Auras are the energy fields around us. Objects and plants also have auras. There are several layers that can be seen by the eye, although not everyone is yet able to see them. The first layer is the etheric layer. The colours that can be seen tell us of a person's mood or well-being.

Crystals are natural semi-precious stones found in the formation of our earth. Crystals have been used for many centuries for healing, jewellery and decoration. I had always felt drawn to the colour of crystals and their formation but never knew to what depth until recently. They are available in all shapes and sizes, and are widely obtainable in most towns and cities.

Oracle cards are guidance cards that are also widely available from bookstores. They give positive guidance and are used for the highest good of the receiver. The card readings can offer support with direction, or guidance if you are confused with an issue, or need assistance with self esteem. The readings I have had from oracle cards have been accurate to my life as you will find out.

Believing is Seeing

Angelic Reiki is a natural and safe healing energy that is passed on to the client through the healer. The energies are 100% pure light which can contribute towards a healthy mind, body and spirit. With this healing system, the Angelic Kingdom pours energy into various and needed parts of the mind, body and soul, where life transformations can take place for the positive.

Chakras are energy centres in the body. There are seven main energy centres and they all have their own symbols and colours. They allow the healing energies to flow to them. The chakras let us know about our well-being. If the chakras are blocked or imbalanced this could lead to ill health.

Past life healing is given to release any traumas from previous lives to enable the recipient to journey through their present life. This healing system is safe as the Angelic Hierarchy guide the healing session.

Seeing is Believing

Below is a diagram of where the chakras are based.

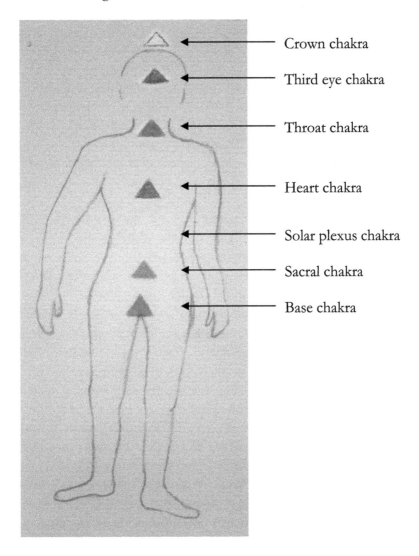

Crown chakra

Third eye chakra

Throat chakra

Heart chakra

Solar plexus chakra

Sacral chakra

Base chakra

The events and occurrences in this book are in chronological order so I will tell you about them just as they developed.

Chapter One

Seeing Is Believing
Believing Is Seeing

In 2005 I became ill. It all began with breathing difficulties and required me to take time off work, but being an avid worker I tried to return to work too soon. I did not want to let down my colleagues.

During my illness of fibromyalgia and chronic fatigue syndrome with breathing difficulties, I spent a lot of money, time and effort to try to recover.

Fibromyalgia, a painful joint and muscle condition, affected most parts of my body. The chronic fatigue was a separate condition, and this was extremely debilitating. I suffered from chronic tiredness, to the point of struggling to visit the toilet. The breathing difficulty was the initial trigger for the illness.

All I wanted to do was to return to my work as a teaching assistant. I also ran a small business which was teaching children about Indian culture. I had spent several years building this up, sometimes working with a couple of hundred children a day.

By July 2006, I was unable to continue employment due to ill health and this was a very traumatic time for me. I was summoned to attend a meeting to discuss my future employment. I have to admit I was terrified. Things were said during this short meeting that I did not agree with. This was the first time I realised I had an out-of-body experience. While we were all sitting in the room, I found that I was looking down on myself, saying to myself that this cannot be happening and that this was not correct. I watched myself without any defence. The things I wanted to say would not come out of my mouth. I now know that this was because I was not fully grounded and my soul had left my physical body. I walked out of the room feeling shocked and shaky. The way I felt I had been treated was all too much as well as the strange out-of-body experience. Perhaps if this had not been such a negative situation I would not have had the outer body experience. As I struggled to accept what had happened with my job, my symptoms worsened.

I now realise that I have had many of these experiences which were quite vivid. When I was a little girl, during my sleep I used to wander or even float down the stairs and I would find myself in the dark and sometimes even walked through the back door. This happened on numerous occasions. I can even remember floating down the road to my aunt's house, in total darkness.

✿✿✿

After many tears of sadness caused by my debilitating condition, and the lack of answers gained from conventional medicine, a friend told me about a spiritual healer that she knew. I decided to make an appointment with this lady, who lived locally as I was now willing to give anything a try, and resolute that my future was not to be helpless and reliant on others. I had always had challenges in my life and I was determined not to give up now. It was just not in my character to give in. Even to this day people have commented on how I have bounced back.

As I was unable to drive, my neighbour took me to see the healer. Dorothea welcomed me in to her house. She could see I was struggling and took me to the healing room upstairs straight away. As I was already very breathless I wondered how I was going to get up the stairs. Every step was difficult, every breath made it harder to take the next step up, my energy became more and more depleted. It was as though I was climbing a mountain.

I was relieved to enter the small cosy room where there was just a bed, a set of drawers and a dream catcher fastened to the ceiling in the corner near the window. Dorothea helped me on to the bed. As I lay down, she asked if I was comfortable but I couldn't move as I was so exhausted, so I just nodded. I didn't know what to expect from this healing session as it was my first time. I became very emotional and cried all the way through the session, not because I was in pain or couldn't breathe but because of the words she spoke.

She told me that something had happened, it was not good and justice would be done. She then said, "They are all here for you. You only had to say yes." Tears just flowed down my face. At this time I thought she was referring to my departed loved ones but I will tell you later who she meant. Dorothea's warm character made me feel very comfortable. She described me as 'mother hen', standing up with my arms stretched out and hundreds of children beneath me. I was also told that a little four year old, blonde haired girl tugged on my clothes and followed me around. She said that when I am sad the little girl is sad, when I cry she cries, when I am happy she is happy. I really didn't know what to make of this. Dorothea went on to explain that the little girl was in the spiritual world. She also told me information about my deceased family. I was given some ideas of herbal medication which I could take to improve my health.

Over the next week I suffered terrible nightmares. I had to do something to stop them as I became so frightened I couldn't sleep. So, I decided to text Dorothea's number for help and received this message:

Sorry destination number format incorrect, valid number prefixes are......
Or from within the U.K.........
This message is free from:
00:00 01-Jan-70

Now this really threw me! There was no time and it was the first day of the year, and the year is 1970, which is the year in which I was born. I just found this very bizarre.

From this day onwards when I have received new text messages usually the new message goes to the top of the New Messages category in my phone, but not with this one. Every other message was below it. This extraordinary message has remained at the top even until today. I have no idea why.

Seeing is Believing

On a warm summer evening in June, sitting at the kitchen table my husband Daren had suggested going to Scotland for a walking trip. He had become a keen walker over the last five years. As he had already been to Scotland before, climbing mountains, he wanted to return to climb more. By now he had accumulated a list of mountains that he wanted to climb. Due to my illness I was unsure as to whether I should accompany him and make my self comfortable in the accommodation just to get away for a while or stay at home. I finally decided I needed a change of scenery, so we started to look for somewhere to stay in the locality of the mountains. Everywhere we telephoned there were no vacancies. Everywhere was booked. We were a little deflated after looking forward to getting away for the summer holidays. We had spent days trying to get a week's accommodation be it a static caravan, a cottage, bed and breakfast or youth hostels. After much searching on the internet we eventually managed to get into 3 youth hostels but would have no accommodation on the Wednesday of that week. Well, I will explain what happened on that Wednesday further on in my journey.

In August 2006, still breathless and unwell, I needed another appointment with Dorothea before going to Scotland so I texted her to see if she had time to see me. She could not fit me in but her advice came to me via text.

"Yes you enjoy Scotland, try and spend time by the streams, rivers, the sea and mountains. Get your feet in clear water to cleanse out."

I had not told Dorothea that I was going to the mountains, I could have been going to the towns or cities. This amazed me.

✿ ✿ ✿

13

On Saturday 12th August we set off for Scotland at five o' clock in the morning. My two younger children, Tristen who was thirteen years old and Alysha who was nine, sat together in the back of the car. Sharon, my eldest who was seventeen did not want to come with us so Paula, who is Daren's cousin, stayed at home with her. Daren already knew he had a long drive ahead of him and wanted to get as far up into Scotland as he could before stopping for a break.

Our first stop was at Aviemore. Daren had promised to take us to the world's best hot chocolate café and we were looking forward to it. The town was full of tourists and we just managed to get a parking space. On reaching the café we were all quite disappointed to find that it was not yet open. Standing outside the café Alysha was prompting us she needed the toilet urgently and this is how we ended up in the café just across the road.

After we had had some refreshments Daren decided to go into the bookshop next door and left me sitting at the table as I was breathless. After some time I decided to go and get some fresh air. I had barely stood still outside the café for a minute when something drew me into the bookshop. At this stage I didn't particularly want to buy or read any books because I had been suffering with blurred vision. I waved to Daren and my children as they were looking at the books. Yet again, Daren was looking at more mountain books! I took my steps gingerly being careful not to waste too much energy. Suddenly, I felt compelled to stop at a section in the bookshop and my hand reached out to a book. I did not know what it was until I looked at the front cover. The book was called, *An Angel Saved My Life* by Jackie Newcomb. Looking up at the sign above the books it read 'Spiritual.' I knew instantly that I wanted to buy the book, and also chose another book from the same section. I walked over to Daren and he was a little surprised but willing to buy the books for me, as I had not been able to read for some time due to my blurred vision. Soon after leaving the shop, I started to read the book whilst drinking my world famous hot chocolate in the café across the road that was now open, I could barely put the book down. I continued to read the book as Daren drove to Torridon. I didn't even glance out of the window to have a look at the scenery as I was so engrossed.

As we approached Torridon, I could see the mountains surrounding us, they seemed dangerously powerful. The height of them was frightening, yet they were beautifully sculptured. We neared the sea loch and eventually arrived at our destination, the youth hostel.

It was very different to anywhere I had ever stayed before. The corridor from the main entrance, led to the stairs down into the kitchen. The large kitchen was well-equipped. Food was labelled by each group of visitors to avoid confusion of belongings. Adjacent to the kitchen was the dining room. There was also a large, comfortable day room with a television and a small quiet room for reading. Our room had a sink, a large wardrobe, a table, a chair and a set of bunk beds. We had never slept in bunk beds as a family before, but we did not mind as we knew we nearly had nowhere to stay at all. Near our room were the shower rooms and the toilets.

Our first evening was exciting as people came in. Two things we noticed were, all the different nationalities within one building and that everyone had a plan for the next day. Daren cautiously planned his first walk for the next morning.

Daren made breakfast for us as he was eager to leave for his walk. He got his gear and set off. I struggled to get out of bed due to the breathlessness and pain in my joints. Tristen and Alysha wanted to go into the television room. I allowed them half an hour to have a bit of space as the rooms were only really adequate for sleeping in. In that time I tried to have some more sleep, hoping I would feel better soon.

As I closed my eyes and lay on the bottom bunk with my duvet huddled up trying to keep warm, I felt a pair of hands cupped over my aching ankles. I instinctively pushed my hand down to my feet to brush them away, not really realising why I was doing this. How on earth could someone be touching my ankles when I was the only person in the room? My heart started to beat faster and I felt somewhat scared. As I moved my hands away it happened again. A little unsure of what to make of this I chose to ignore it. Then the children returned. I decided to get up and make myself a hot drink. We then sat in the quiet room with a book each. As I continued to read Jackie Newcomb's book I asked the children if they wanted to listen to some of the stories. They listened with enthusiasm and wanted to hear more of these miraculous stories.

I then told the children I was going to ask for a sign from the angels. I asked the angels if they were really there for me, and if so, to give me a sign with a feather or a coin. Afterwards I remembered to thank the angels.

Later that evening we went to the local restaurant. I pulled myself up to sit on a high stool at the bar and Daren stood by me. After a short time we moved as we were in the way of the waitresses and we sat a little further away. Tristen and Alysha told Daren that I had asked for a sign from the angels. When Daren heard Alysha say I had asked for a coin he instinctively looked at where I had been sitting and under the high stool was a twenty pence piece. We looked at each other in amazement. I told Daren that there was definitely nothing under that stool before I sat there because I had bent down to get up on to it.

We were now wondering if this was the sign. I was very excited as I picked up the coin as this was what I had asked for. Whilst we sat contemplating what had just happened, we shared thoughts about this strange occurrence.

Soon after, I began to feel sceptical. I doubted this was a sign from the angels, as we were in a sociable environment. I decided to ask for another sign just to confirm what was found.

We returned to the hostel where we relaxed and I read more of my book. When we retired to our room, there was a feeling of togetherness as we chatted before falling asleep. During the night I woke up to see lights in the room. There were 3 at the back of the room and one by my head. I rested my head on the pillow again thinking Daren had simply put his head lamp on to lead him to the toilets that were in the corridor.

Seeing is Believing

The following day Daren's second climb was to Liatach and this time Tristen wanted to join him. Tristen had previously climbed Snowdon, Scafell Pike, Ben Nevis and other mountains before the age of eleven, so he was quite experienced for his age. However, this did not stop me from worrying as it has only got to be a slip of the foot for an accident to happen. As much as I enjoy the mountains, I also appreciate the dangers they hold.

Daren drove to the bottom of the mountain, as Alysha and I sat in the car watching them take their path up as far as our eyes could see. After an hour of watching them disappearing into the distance, we decided to go and sit by the loch as it was a sunny day.

We sat eating sandwiches on the grass, opposite the village shop, watching the clouds go over the mountain across the loch. We had never seen dragon flies so close to us before, they just wouldn't leave us alone. Alysha kept screaming and running away from them. Even Morag the lady in the shop came out to see what was going on! You see Torridon is usually a quiet little place, where everyone knows everyone and it is so peaceful.

After enjoying our gorgeous sunny day we returned to the hostel. A guest had come into the hostel for the night. Her name was Heidi and she informed me that she was a kindergarten teaching assistant from Germany. We had a cup of tea and played a game of scrabble as Alysha became a little bored. After the game we all decided to read to pass some time away. As I opened my book the next story was about a girl called Heidi. I looked out of the window to the left of me where Heidi had been sitting. What a coincidence I thought.

I closed the book to allow myself some time to absorb this. I then sat there thinking of Georgia, a little girl who plays with Alysha. A couple of minutes later I randomly opened a page, the story in front of me was about a little girl called Georgia. How could this happen again so soon? Another coincidence?

Heidi had got her keys to the room and that was the last time I saw her.

The Helpful Stranger

A few hours had passed. Alysha was in the big lounge flicking through the television channels. The hostel owner was in the kitchen cleaning the fridge as I made myself a cup of tea. She stood there with a dishcloth in her hand looking quite tired, complaining about the food not being labelled, making it aware to me that a marker was provided and the instructions were on the wall. She complained that she did not like to throw food away as it was so wasteful. Then she asked me if I wanted a pack of cheese as it had no name an on it. I gladly took this as I have the same outlook that food should not be wasted. It would have been put in the bin otherwise as room needed to be made for the newly arriving guests. As she continued to empty more unlabelled items from the fridge, she came across a can of lager and from behind me a gentle looking old man appeared. She asked the man if he wanted the drink. He replied in a soft voice that it would be lovely. Without paying too much attention to him he had left the kitchen and went down into the lounge.

I then suddenly thought of Alysha being on her own with a complete stranger.

As I made my way down the few stairs I could hear the man talking to her. I asked Alysha if she was all right. She said that the man had seen Daren and Tristen on the mountain. I was a little surprised to hear this as he seemed too old to climb it. I assumed he probably saw us altogether as a family at some point.

The man had appeared to look like Santa Claus but without the beard. His white hair was combed to perfection, with electric blue eyes and slightly rosy cheeks. He wasn't very tall and he had a lovely warm feeling about him.

He started to tell me he had seen Daren and Tristen at the top of the mountain. I asked him what time he saw them and he replied that it was in the morning. He also said they should be on their way down by now. He said that Daren and Tristen did not think they would see deer on the mountain top, but there were deer in the area. He got his digital camera out to show me. What I saw was a beautiful picture of two stags on a mountain range in the clouds. It was quite a close up photograph. It was just so gorgeous that I could not stop complimenting the view in the photograph. The very first thought that came to my mind was Adam and Eve in Heaven. I don't know why I thought that, perhaps because it was so natural and the beauty of it was overwhelming. I don't think I have ever felt so overwhelmed by a snapshot. As this gentle man put his camera away I asked again what time he saw Daren. He didn't give me a time but he did say they should be down now. As he stood and drank his beer, I sat on the arm chair close to the very large window. The window was from floor to ceiling which let in a vast amount of natural light and complimented the amazing view. Some ten to fifteen minutes had now passed and there was still no sign of Daren and Tristen, I was starting to get worried as they had been out walking for seven hours. Daren estimated six hours when I asked for the time for their return. I think the man could sense the worry that I was feeling. He said, "If you are worried why don't you go and meet them?" I looked up at him and sighed as I felt quite exhausted. I replied that I might do, but I didn't budge, because I couldn't right then. The man had left the room and as I still sat fixed to the armchair, I watched him drive off in his electric blue car, thinking nothing of this.

Alysha was quite happy watching television whilst I gazed out of the window. After a while Alysha was complaining she was hungry, I promised her we would have something to eat after we picked up her dad and brother from the bottom of the mountain. She waited patiently.

We got in the car and drove to where Daren said he would come down from the mountain. As we neared the mountainside I saw a car parked in a passing point. Lo and behold, who was sitting in the car? Yes, it was the gentle old man. As I pulled up next to him I wound my window down and said, "Hello." He replied, "I thought I'd save you the trouble of coming out." I thanked him for it, and I went on to say, "I know I shouldn't worry but I can't help it." He replied, "I know you can't help worrying." The man was speaking to me as if he had known me for years. I pulled up behind him as this was a single track road and got out of the car. It was now approaching evening and there were a lot of midges in the mild air. As we stood by his car talking to him we were getting terribly bitten. We were wafting them with our hands away from our faces. The man and I looked up at the mountain to see if we could see them, I said to him that they weren't even wearing anything bright so they could be noticed. He also commented how important it was to wear high visibility clothing. I told him it was like looking for a needle in a haystack. He replied, "Yes, it is." Alysha stood at the side of me complaining of the midges biting her, so I said to the man we would sit and wait in the car for another twenty minutes. I thanked him for coming out to look for my family. He said he would wait at the hostel in case they came back another route.

There was still no sign of them so we headed back to the hostel. As I pulled up in the car park the man got out of his car. He knew my concerns had deepened and as I repeated that I can not help worrying. He said once again, "I know you can't help but worry." I told him I would check with the wardens in the office as now they had gone past eight hours and there was no return. I noticed the man had the same book as Daren in his car and all his walking gear, but then again it was a popular book for all highland walkers.

Alysha and I fought the midges off to get into the building, I queried about the distance of the walk and possible routes down. The warden had said there was no need to send for a search team as they usually allow ten hours before raising any alarms. I suppose I had to take his word, although he did point out to me another area where they could come down, but it would be a long exhausting walk back so I would need to drive up to them.

By now Alysha was quite hungry. I made a point of getting her some food before going out looking again.

As we sat at the dining table in the corner of the large dining room I looked up and saw Daren and Tristen at the top of the stairs. I got up as quick as I could with a big sigh of relief. I hugged them and told them how worried I had been. As they were just as hungry as we were they went straight to the showers to get washed. Alysha was just as happy as I was to see them back. We all sat at the table having our evening meal and I began telling Daren our accounts of the day. As I spoke of the gentle old man, Daren said he had met him towards the top of the mountain and he found it very strange to see him so high up because of his age. Besides, he was on his way down and Daren and Tristen were on their way up. They confirmed that they did have a brief discussion about the mountain deer. I also told Daren how this man had been out to look for them to save me the hassle. Daren then said it was this man who brought them back just now and drove as if he was twenty years old, swerving round the corner. Daren explained how the man had mentioned to him that he used to love mountain walking with his mate who had now passed away.

A few minutes later I saw the man coming down the last few stairs. I immediately invited him over so we could thank him. He walked over to where we were sitting. I told him how grateful I was and asked him to join us for a glass of wine. He spoke gently and very calmly, with a great presence all around him. He replied, "I've had one for today, thank you." Daren asked where he was going tomorrow. The man replied quite simply, "Oh I don't know." Before saying goodbye he left us with an overall glow of warm loving feeling. As soon as he left the room we reflected on what he said. Everyone had a plan for the next day, people usually knew exactly where they were going, which walk or mountain they were going to climb. People we briefly spoke to were pleasant enough, although nobody really bothered about anybody else, people just got on with their own. It all just seemed unreal. So why did this man go to the lengths he did just for us? That was the last time we saw him.

As we settled in our room I asked Daren why he had put his head lamp on to visit the toilet the night before, he replied that he did go to the toilet but did not have his head lamp on. I insisted he stopped being silly and that he did. He insisted he did not wear his head lamp. As I started to get a cold shudder I went towards him to cuddle up, becoming eerily unsettled. The children were still awake, looking at each other in a confused and frightened manner. We huddled up together. I then started to explain that I was awake the previous night and pointed out that I had seen these lights and they appeared to be slightly bigger than the size of tennis balls. This was now really bizarre because at that moment we could not logically explain it. I don't know how the others slept but I felt a little scared!

The Hitchhikers

After we finished our breakfast, the children wandered off to the lounge. A lot of the travellers had already left for the day. As we sat at the breakfast table taking our time, for some reason I kept staring at the back rest on the chair. What was drawing me to the chair I could not quite understand at first and then it dawned on me that I could actually see wings. As I turned my head around to look at all of the other chairs they also had this beautiful carving. Daren agreed with me that they looked like a shape of wings, although not quite sharing the excitement I was feeling. I just felt at this moment in time that this was confirmation. Confirmation the angels were near me.

We cleared our table and went back to the room to gather our belongings to move on to our next destination. We had booked to come back for another couple of nights later on in the week.

We drove towards Loch Maree it was on the road to Gairloch. I wanted to stop at the loch to put my feet in the water to cleanse, just like Dorothea had mentioned. As we drove towards the loch along the long straight road there was little traffic. The entrance to the loch was on the right hand side, standing opposite was a man and a boy thumbing to hitch a lift. From a distance the man appeared to be the boy's father, they both had fair hair.

My intuition was telling me we needed to stop the car. We had to give them a lift. The others in the car said we could not as they were strangers but I had an inner feeling that it would be fine. As Daren indicated to turn to the loch I wound down my window and asked them where they wanted to go. They replied they wanted to get to Gairloch and Ullapool. We were surprised they were heading for the same places as us. I told them to wait a few minutes while we visited the loch then we would come back to pick them up. As the car started to turn down the loch road the man at the side of the road shouted not to go down there as the road was not safe, he shouted with such urgency. The man told us to go a little further back to the next turn which was safe. As Daren continued turning I also shouted, 'Don't go down that road!' I think Daren became irate as he didn't want to drive back on himself, even though it was not that far away.

It was only a quick visit at the loch. We took our shoes and socks off and went in to wet our feet. I immediately felt very calm and relaxed and had an overall sense of well-being, gazing into the beauty of this magnificently still loch.

As we left, Daren drove up the track we had been advised not to use. Driving up we noticed a danger sign hanging upside down. I pointed this out as it seemed like a bad omen. Daren assured me we would be fine. Further on, the track became overgrown and the surface was broken. I was very concerned about the road. It was clearly unsafe I urged Daren to go back the way we had come but he insisted we could make it. It was a slow and precarious journey.

When we reached the main road the man and boy were no longer there. We were puzzled. They must have got a lift from someone else. As we talked we realised they had no luggage and no coats. This was unusual in this area, as nearly everyone had rucksacks and rain coats in Scotland as the forecast was rain for most of the week. We continued along the road to Gairloch arriving at lunchtime. It was a very small fishing village but we never saw the man and boy either along the road or when we arrived. Even when we arrived at Ullapool there was no sign of them. I am sure even to this day that when we made that turn to drive further up, I looked in Daren's wing mirror and I could not see them.

My thoughts now were who were these people? Were they really in this physical world? Were they human angels to warn us and get us out of danger?

Little Light

After driving for hours to get to Talisker on the Isle of Skye we realised we were going to have trouble finding somewhere to stay. This was the Wednesday we had no where to stay and everywhere had 'No Vacancy' signs up. Daren saw an inn and decided to ask if there was any chance of a room. The landlord said he would check but was doubtful. As he looked at his reservations book he asked how many the room would be for. He looked up surprised and said unbelievably there was a room available. He explained to Daren that they had been fully booked the previous week and would be the following week. They were always fully booked as it was a tourist area and the height of the holiday season. Was it pure luck that on this particular night they had a family room for four?

The accommodation turned out to be a small bungalow situated on the edge of the loch. After we had settled we went over to the inn for dinner. It was very busy and we had to wait a while. Finally, a table became available and we ordered the children's meals. Alysha drank a glass of coke on an empty stomach and soon started to feel unwell. Daren took her out for some fresh air leaving us. Tristen was sitting opposite me at the table. As I looked up I saw a small ball of fluttering light hovering above where Alysha had been sitting. I was speechless as I sat watching the light I was sure I could see a fast fluttering of wings. I was aware of Tristen asking what was wrong but I could not speak, not because I was breathless, but because I was shocked. The fluttering ball of light only lasted a few seconds. I looked around the room to see if there was anything that could have reflected the light but there was nothing. When the others returned I whispered to Daren I had just seen a fairy and he said he wasn't surprised after what had been happening.

Seeing is Believing

The next day we left and drove back towards Torridon. It was a clear, dry day but cold. I sat in the car with my coat fastened to keep warm, which I struggled to do. We drove past a large rocky area and I could clearly see two wolves sculpted into the surface. At this time I was breathless and could not make anyone aware of them as we approached them. As we neared the wolves, they disappeared and I could only see two huge rocks. At this time I smiled to myself. I knew they were there for just me to see as now I realised it was part of my spiritual journey.

✿✿✿

Daren had decided to take the children for a short woodland walk and on leaving the car I called Alysha back and told her to look out for the fairies in the forest. On returning forty five minutes later Daren and the children looked surprised as they informed me that in the forest was a hillock with a plaque before it which did indeed say that the hillock is where the fairies dwell. The children were surprised as to how I knew about the fairies, as I had never been to those woodlands before. I can only say that I was given prior information about the woodlands by intuition.

✿✿✿

We stopped for lunch at a small café. I had read the headlines of a newspaper reporting on the death of two small children and I was feeling deeply saddened when a feeling of complete calm came over me. When I stood to leave I found another coin under my seat. This was not there when I sat down and I believe it was a sign from the Angels that coincided with my feeling of calm.

Going Home

After a lovely change of scenery in Scotland, filled with strange occurrences, it was time to make our journey home. I was sitting in the car relaxing, just looking out of the window when I saw an angel. It was in a cloud formation. She appeared from a side view, her head tilting forwards, one knee bent higher than the other and her arms flowing behind her. She was finely shown in white with the green forest immediately behind her. Amazed at how clearly she appeared I found it difficult to believe what I was seeing. Yet again I was breathless and fatigued so I could not tell any of my family to look and see what I could see. I could see it so clearly, it was definitely there, another sign. I was truly surprised even though I had previously seen figures in the clouds of lions and bulls.

When we arrived home we were all allocated jobs as everyone was tired.

Tristen cleaned out the car and found a small pure white feather under Daren's seat. I felt the angels were keeping us safe on our long journey home as we all had a dreadful night's sleep at a youth hostel the previous night. The feather was no surprise to me as I was now even more thankful and acknowledged that the angels were there for my family and me.

Chapter Two

Visiting the Angel Shop

After telling Paula about my experiences she told me about an angel shop that had opened nearby. I knew I had to visit it, Paula also came along for the day.

As soon as I entered the shop I felt a warm glow come over me and a sense of, I suppose, you could say love. This warm glow made me feel wonderful. I instantly knew this was a comforting place. Paula had already become emotional as she said she always did in this shop. Once there, I was drawn to a particular area and saw a small beautifully painted plaque. As I looked more closely I realised everything I had seen in Scotland was there in this painting: the wolves, lions, and rainbows, the wild flowers, another sign of my spiritual journey.

While at the shop I bought some healing stones. As I paid for them I spoke to the assistant whose name was Faith, which I thought was totally ideal. She told me that the Archangels gathered there. She could tell I had become quite excited as I continued to ask more about them. I then walked around the shop looking up towards the ceiling hoping to see them. Well I could try, I thought to myself!

When I got home I found a leaflet in the bag of stones that I bought, it was advertising an Angelic Reiki Course.

By now I was pretty sure that the angels were there to help me, after finding feathers in the garage and in various rooms in the house too. This was confirmation.

Could the angels even be there to find lost objects? Read on and you'll soon find out.

I had lost an important letter that I needed for the next morning and in desperation I looked everywhere. Because it was not in the place I thought I had put it I decided to ask for help from the angels. The next morning I found it in the drawer that I had already searched in, it was right on the very top. I told my family in excitement, almost like a child. I was sure to thank the angels for their unconditional support.

A Memory

I sat in my living room gazing out of the window when a past memory popped into my mind from nine years ago. The memory was about what happened after I gave birth to Alysha. I had a traumatic pregnancy and birth, which left me with a dysfunctional pelvis resulting in excruciating pain.

I remembered passing out in Daren's arms. Throughout this time I suffered no pain and all I could see was whiteness whilst I was unconscious. The white was whiter than any white I had ever seen. I felt warm and carefree, it was just so serene. I can remember enjoying the feeling until I came back with the alarming pain.

I sat wondering, is this what the feeling is like when you experience near death? Strangely I felt things were starting to slot into place. Just like the feelings of being held down when I have been in bed, wide awake calling for help and yet unable to move and no one can hear me. Having had many of these experiences, some pleasant and some not, I was beginning to understand they were all happening for a reason. It could have been as simple as holding me down to tell me that I should not be in a certain situation.

Insight

The ever growing presence in my bedroom made me feel secure, happy and loved. The fairies that I could see were maybe a couple of inches high and slim with their continuous fluttering of the wings. This was the same night that Daren had a nightmare. He said I calmed him down. He said this on a number of occasions but I could not remember saying a thing.

28

✿✿✿

Sitting in the conservatory with Daren and Alysha reading, I looked out and saw in the sky a very clear shape of a hand with each finger visible. Above the hand was a feather. Alysha agreed that she could see exactly the same. My intuition was telling me to receive the help from the angels.

✿✿✿

It was shortly after the Scotland trip that I became aware I was feeling other people's symptoms, anything from muscle strain to headaches to nausea.

Coincidences?

We had gone out for the day to the local forest. Daren had taken the children off for a bike ride as I sat in the car reading. I turned round to see if someone was sitting behind me because I kept feeling a presence. As I read the word rainbow in my book a song on the radio came on simultaneously it was 'Somewhere over the Rainbow.' I looked out of the window a little puzzled, thinking this was a coincidence.

Later, I read the words 'love yourself 'and the next song I heard on the radio was 'I love you.' It was a very old song, by an artist I did not recognise. I was beginning to think this was not really happening.

I decided to have a change from the radio and put on a compact disc, I quite happily had the music on in the background as I continued to read the next chapter which was about meditation. As I read the word 'meditation' the compact disc player turned off. I decided to try the meditation as I knew now that these were not coincidences, they were all valid messages. I was only brought back after ten minutes by the children knocking on the window. The book said 'meditate for just ten minutes.' Coincidences ?

✿ ✿ ✿

Sitting at home in my conservatory as Sharon, my eldest daughter stood talking to me, I went into a daze. I looked up and something caught my eye. It appeared to look like an angel in the bricks and mortar. My mouth dropped open, Sharon instantly glanced to see what I could see and smiled. She agreed she could clearly see an angel. This could have been a simple blob of cement but what was clear was a definite shape. It was a shape of an angel.

✿ ✿ ✿

Ever since seeing angels in cloud formations, angel wings in my bedroom at night, receiving angelic guidance and other help from the angels we also heard tapping on the window at night and tapping on wood which frightened both the children and me at first. After reassuring the children it was not too much of a problem and that it could be solved, they were calm about this situation. It became apparent to me that this was due to my channels being open.

My way of explaining this would be that as I was on this spiritual journey, naturally I had become a channel for spiritual service. As a person channels, they become a vessel for vibrational frequency which can be passed down from the spiritual realms and guides. I felt that other spirits were also contacting me as a way of communication. At this time it was out of control. With the help of a colleague we managed to stop the tapping.

Healing

I thought I could try giving Daren healing for snoring and nervous twitches that he gets when he is relaxing. I was amazed to see that the healing worked which meant a good night's sleep for me!

Talking to my neighbour Marlene, she complained that her partner was such a bad snorer she had not had a good night's sleep for years, and it was starting to become more of a problem. I offered to help by sending some distant healing. She accepted, not knowing what to expect and soon forgot about the conversation.

The next morning, I asked how she had slept. She replied very well, she had slept right through the night, commenting that her partner had not snored. It was at this point that she remembered our previous conversation. She stood open mouthed for a moment before saying the healing had worked and thank you. Even though I had done some healing on Daren, I was still amazed to see the result with Mike.

✿ ✿ ✿

A few days later I was talking with another friend who also had a snoring husband. She was aware of my angelic happenings as well as my 'out of the blue' healing abilities. She asked if I had done anything for her husband because for the previous few nights he had not been snoring! I said no but then realised that the two husbands shared the same name and I had unknowingly healed two in one!

Never Got To Say Goodbye

This particular day I had spent time with a friend. She began telling me about her visit to Greece and during her time out there her grandma had passed away and she did not get to say goodbye. It was naturally heartbreaking for her to talk about this. An hour later another friend of ours came to bring my daughter back from her house as her daughter and Alysha were friends at school. After reading her oracle cards she sat in the same chair as my other friend and started telling me about her granddad. She told me that she went to Greece for her holiday and in that time abroad her granddad had passed away and she never got to say goodbye. This was déjà vu, had I not just heard this same story an hour earlier? I instantly knew she was going to say the words 'I didn't get to say goodbye', I leapt up from the chair with my hands on my head shouting, "I can't believe this." It was unbelievable.

The Spa Vouchers

Another similar occurrence was when my neighbour told me she was having a day of pampering treatment at a health spa and then another friend had also said the same and the stories were that they had both misplaced their vouchers for about a year and recently found them, they were both coincidently going to use them in the same week at the same spa. Funnily they both lived in the same road as me.

Chapter Three

Course Confirmation

After the episodes of the angelic healing leaflets being put in my bags repeatedly, I was urged to ring Rosemary, the course facilitator, to enquire about the course. When I told her I was unwell, she encouraged me even more so to go ahead with the course. The price for her course added up to a 9 and then, divided by 3, displayed 3. This number was, The Trinity to Divine Truth. I had read the number three was of spiritual significance in an angel book. My heart beat became faster with an over whelming feeling of joy as I knew that this was leading to something. I felt excited to do the course but was a little doubtful due to my health, wondering if I could manage even an hour, never mind two and a half days. Because my urges were too strong I could not ignore them but needed time to think.

Meeting the Authors

Reading the previously mentioned book by Jackie Newcomb I felt I had to meet her. I sat talking to my neighbour, Marlene, and told her how much I wanted to meet Jackie. Two weeks later there I was sitting on the front seat diagonally opposite her at a 'Second Sight' night. I was very excited as I sat with my friends and family. There were two other authors present, Jean Kelford and Glennyce Eckersley, each gave a twenty minute introduction about themselves and their books. Their talks were interesting. I sat there nodding, as I could relate to what was being said. The floor was then opened to the audience for questions, comments and experiences. The atmosphere in the room was quite sombre as there were a lot of people grieving and I suppose they had come for confirmation about their loved ones. Paula reminded me that I had the opportunity to speak about my experiences. I raised my hand feeling quite nervous, my heart had not beaten this fast for nearly a year. I felt I had just been on the treadmill. With the nerves and the excitement mixed together I held on to the microphone and spoke directly to Jackie Newcomb. I explained what had happened to me and how I thoroughly enjoyed the feeling of the angels around me. I expressed to the authors and the audience how I felt as if I was flying high with the angels. I went on to tell everyone how I had started healing, I wanted to know if I should continue using these newly acquired healing abilities and the other two authors said I should and see where it would lead.

The room seemed to have lit up with love. I felt as though I could have talked forever, I also felt proud of myself as I had not talked in front of a crowd this big for a good year or so. It was a good confidence boost.

Angel Blessings

After another visit to the angel shop I received yet another leaflet on Angelic Reiki. I had started buying more angel guidance cards and used them to find and understand the path I was meant to take. As this was Sharon's first visit to the shop she became overwhelmed and sobbed uncontrollably. She was comforted by Faith and I, although Sharon had no idea why she was so tearful.

Every time I bought items from the angel shop the assistants put a hand full of angel blessings in the bag, which I thought rounded off the trip to the shop just perfectly, a lovely gesture. We were now ready for a coffee and yet again I found another penny behind my chair.

When we arrived home I had put a few of the angel blessings on my bedroom window sill just in a pile. I was now used to seeing angel and fairy wings when I closed my eyes and an advance to this was bright white light and love hearts: every time I got a warm loving feeling.

When I awoke I found to my amazement that the angel blessings that I had left in a small pile had mysteriously formed into a circle, I instantly started to ask the family if they had done this, but how could they? They were all fast asleep in their beds. The circle was so perfect!

Blessings in circle

The next day when Sharon went into my room, she shouted frantically for us to go up the stairs, we thought it was something serious. When we arrived in the room we saw that the angel blessings had rearranged themselves again and one of the angels had moved lower. The shape now looked like an angel if you looked invertedly. What I had noticed also was that there were nine angel blessings. 9 divided by 3 equals 3 and again 3 is The Trinity to Divine Truth.

Angel in blessings

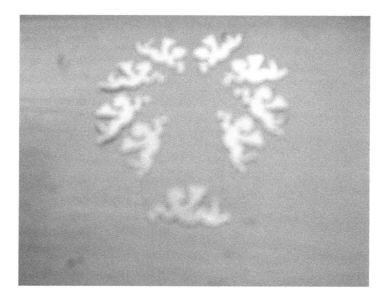

Ariel

Later that day I decided to find the name of my Guardian Angel, asking for the sign to be a feather. At the same time Alysha was playing with a mermaid doll. She had not bothered playing with her for over a year but today she put wings on the doll and then drew her. She made three pictures, all the same, of the doll with wings. Knowing that three is a sacred number I paid more attention. The doll was called Ariel, also the name of an Archangel. My answer was given and confirmed when, after leaving the doll and coming back to it a minute later, we found a small pure white feather lying on its chest. That night I had a message from the angels saying that they loved Alysha and at the same time I had the presence of both angel and fairy wings around me. My whole self felt warmed and aglow.

The Healing Course

I had now booked to do the Angelic Reiki Course though I was still unsure as to whether I could actually complete it or not. My intuition and gut feelings were that I would. This was again confirmed as I kept seeing 252 on the digital clock which was the fee of this course. By adding all the numbers and dividing into 3 the final number was again 3, The Trinity to Divine Truth.

The number three is a very important number for me as I have mentioned earlier. After deciding that I was going to commit my self to the Angelic Reiki Course I was told there would be four ladies attending, coincidently one was unable to attend. Then there were only three of us. All three of us had three children each.

Rosemary was the course facilitator. She had a lovely relaxed demeanour. She was welcoming, warm and made sure we were comfortable. Rosemary had a boxer dog, which I have to admit I was terrified of as I have had a couple of bad experiences in my life with dogs. Telsa was huge but elderly and therefore I tried to justify that she would do me no harm.

I had met the other two ladies for the very first time.

Caroline had lovely big deep brown eyes. She appeared confident, loving and caring. Whilst in her presence for that short time I noticed she was a talkative and a knowledgeable person. Her features actually resembled a picture of a Celtic woman on a compact disc that I listened to regularly.

Lyn, the other lady seemed reserved in character, but nevertheless pleasant, gentle and warm. She spoke very calmly, almost as though she had no cares or worries.

I can remember saying to all three women that we most probably had already met in another life. All of us agreed as we nodded our heads, smiling. Everyone seemed lovely. What a great start.

The first part of the course went smoothly. I walked away feeling lighter and clearer within my own body. I just felt that some sort of healing had taken place already.

Driving home I felt so confident that the journey passed quickly and I soon arrived home. As soon as I had greeted my family I went upstairs. Drawn to the window I looked again in amazement to find the angel blessings had moved from a circle to a parting, making a clear divide. It was strange to see that this had happened in a couple of hours and yet again, nobody had touched them. What did this mean?

It was a sleepless night. The word 'north' and number '12' were inscribed in my minds eye. In my bedroom there was a photograph of a pyramid mountain in Scotland, it was clearly showing me 'a third eye with an angel behind it.' The third eye is one of the energy centres in spiritual terms, it is found between the eyebrows.

Now that it was the second day of the course I woke up feeling enthusiastic. As Daren drove me there I felt more and more breathless, I wanted to ask him to take me back home. Something kept urging me to stay focused, as I should not turn away from doing the course.

When we arrived I steadily made my way in. Daren and the children followed me into the hallway, making a fuss of Telsa as she greeted everyone. Alysha noticed the angel figurines. I could feel her excitement as she looked around, soon after Daren and the children left.

Not long after my family left, I felt so emotional that I broke down in tears. Yes I was unwell but it seemed to be a cry of relief. As I leaned over the kitchen work surface Rosemary comforted me, she rubbed my back and I felt a sense of calmness washing over me.

Telsa the dog had also come to me standing at my feet. She was also telling me everything would be all right. I suppose she was reassuring me.

I also felt the amazing love of the angels and their presence in this room. I was so emotional that I could not make conversation with anyone at that moment.

I lay on Rosemary's sofa with tears rolling down my cheeks as she started the next part of the course. At this time I wondered if this was unpleasant for Lyn and Caroline as I did not want to spoil their experience of the course. But I could not help how I was feeling.

I managed to sit up during break time for a cup of tea. I knew these ladies were very understanding as we chatted. I laughingly said to them we were meant to be together on this course for a reason, whether we liked it or not. My intuition was strongly sending this message as I sat discussing other relevant information in my life recently.

A few days earlier I had a dream. It was in 3 parts.

The first part was this; a lady pulling things out of my body, although at the time I had no idea of what she was removing. It was a vivid dream, as I woke up with physical pain in my stomach. During the second part of the dream a lady stood in front of me, I was shouting 'bring me down, bring me down,' I was floating towards the ceiling, my feelings were clearly unsettled at this time.

The third part of the dream showed me being reunited with my deceased family and friends at a party. This part of the dream was very real to me too as I can remember touching them and they were in the physical body.

At this healing session we were now ready to practise healing on one another. Because we had an odd number one of us practised on Telsa.

After our short practise Lyn gave some feedback on what she felt whilst healing me. She started describing how she was spiritually removing something from my body. At first I just sat and listened then I had a flashback of the dream. Yes, it was Lyn who was taking the things out of my body through spiritual healing. I spoke out loudly about how I had already dreamt of this happening. I was in a little bit of shock trying to make sense of it as I stuttered with my speech. I then went on to say there was more to the dream but Rosemary asked me not to say anymore until something else came up during the day.

I was now quite excited and anticipated what would happen next.

We changed partners. This healing practise was now becoming peculiar. I felt as if Caroline was floating. It was a feeling of sitting on a ship swaying from side to side. When we had feedback I was told that I was not grounded. She had felt I was levitating and needed to bring me down. Now I did shout out in excitement that this was another part of my dream! Well, now I was convinced that dreams can come true.

During our lunch break I told the ladies how things had been moving in the house and there seemed to be a link with things happening to me. I also explained about the mountain picture in the bedroom, how I could see the third eye and an angel behind it. Well this was making sense, as we had invoked the angels and used our third eye for healing this day. I was now starting to think that what ever I saw, be it in dreams or in objects, it was coming true. I was living it. How could this be?

After a lovely day learning to heal I was quite tired and ready for a good nights rest. As I lay in bed, I struggled to sleep. The house was quiet with everyone else fast asleep. I eventually drifted off, but awoke to find myself levitating. I think the shock of finding myself off the bed did not help. I must have been off the bed a couple of inches. As soon as I realised this I grabbed hold of Daren asking him to hold on to me, hoping he could help. I panicked and did not know how to resolve the levitating. A few minutes passed which seemed a long time, then I felt safe and fell in to a deep sleep.

On the third day, I awoke feeling very positive, calm and relaxed, almost like a brand new person. The sun was shining on this mid-September morning, the air still warm and pleasant. I set off a little early so that I could speak to Rosemary by herself. Driving down the single carriageway I put on a Celtic compact disc and for some reason I cried most of my journey there. The music and songs were naturally inspiring and touching and I felt very connected to the angels. One part of the lyrics on the disc was 'I've just stepped in to see you on, I'll only stay a while, I want to see how you're getting on.' My heart pounded as I wiped my tears away. The tears were of joy, happiness and privilege of experiencing the moment and the presence of the angels.

Arriving at Rosemary's, Telsa had come to greet me yet again on my final day of the course. Considering how fearful I had been all my life of dogs, I felt absolutely fine with her. Rosemary had been busy cleansing the room. I apologised for arriving early then explained that I felt an urge to do so. She welcomed me in as usual, with a warm loving hug. She complimented me on how well I looked. I told Rosemary that I felt lighter in my body and mind and how I could now see clearly, my sight was crystal clear. The room was fresh for the day's work and the kettle was on the boil. As we stood in the kitchen I told Rosemary about the levitating in the night. She was very helpful and gave me guidance. She told me I needed to make sure I was grounded with the help of the angels.

We spoke about how my changes would affect the family and that I should do my best not to neglect them, as this is how they could feel. I would need to explain to them that many spiritual changes would take place. She also reminded me they would in return need to bear my changes in mind and accept what happens. I took a deep sigh as I could feel there would be transformation for us all. It would be positive, that I knew for sure.

Caroline and Lyn arrived, we met with hugs. Telsa made sure she was not going to miss out on any of the fuss. We all in turn patted her on the head and spoke to her as we sat sipping our tea.

Soon into the attunement, I felt a hand touch my knee. I went on to visualise very clearly a Victorian scene. In a room there was a big wooden bed with a wooden headboard. Above the headboard was a dark wooden shelf matching the bed. The white bed linen was obvious to the eye. On the shelf there were ornaments which were at a distance and therefore I am unable to describe them in detail, however they seemed to be made from pottery. I could see a girl, about eight years of age, dressed in a white pinafore dress and a white frilly hat. She walked towards the bed and then the visual closed down.

I did wonder whether that was a past life. Why else would I have been shown it?

It was now time to heal our partner, Telsa was mine. She seemed quite comfortable lying on the floor in the sun.

We were going to do healing with Ascended Masters. In Rosemary's living room was a picture of Jesus Christ and often throughout my time on this course I was drawn to it, I felt it was calling me. I had selected Jesus Christ prior to the healing as my Ascended Master. I have always felt closeness with this Master though I had no concept of how much.

During this powerful session Jesus was present. He touched my head and I sobbed as I could not control my emotions yet again. The warm loving glow was all around me. The overwhelming emotions I was going through were almost indescribable. I was sobbing to the degree of disturbing the others but the more I was trying to stop myself, the more I was choked. I felt a hand touch the crown of my head. I continued to weep for another ten minutes or so until the healing session was brought to a close. How could I hide my emotions of love, blessings and happiness for this great healer? My intuition told me I had been blessed. I just knew it, Jesus had touched my head. This was a very powerful, moving and extraordinary experience.

We then had another session and the same presence of Jesus was there. Now I had gained the experience of healing energies of the angels as well as Jesus Christ, this was overwhelming to say the least. As a person who has her own beliefs and outlook on life, this truly was an amazing time of my life.

I have always looked up to Jesus, be it through dramas, films or pictures. I believe it does not matter which colour or religion a person is to have a belief, there is free choice to believe in more than one guru, saint or healer. Just as people believe in God in different religions, in their own traditions, still there is only one God.

Seeing is Believing

We had completed the course and had learned various forms of healing, which was exciting and wonderful. It was time to say our goodbyes and we all decided to keep in touch as we all felt this was important.

Chapter Four

Earth Angel?

The next day Marlene, my neighbour and friend asked if I wanted to visit the angel shop. Her friend wanted to go to the shop as it was much talked about just lately due to my strange experiences and I suppose because of their own interests. I went along with them.

As soon as the shop had opened we went in. Faith the shop assistant was rather surprised to see me walk in, as the oracle cards I had ordered had arrived two minutes earlier. She explained how she was just about to phone me to collect them. We looked at each other and shrugged our shoulders almost as if to say, 'Oh, OK, whatever.' I had become quite friendly with Faith. I viewed her as a younger sister and she reminded me of a fairy with her kind and gentle nature. That was it, her new nickname would be Faith Fairy.

Whilst the other two ladies were wandering in the shop I stood talking to Faith. I told her how I had always felt different from everyone and I was also called 'the black sheep of the family.' I admit it was not pleasant to hear that being said about me, but I now realise why.

I have always wanted to help people. I can remember sitting on the train and a young student couldn't stop coughing. Spontaneously, I rummaged in my bag to find a chewing gum so that it would calm the cough. I passed her the gum and the cough calmed down, she seemed surprised but grateful. Sometimes it's the simplest acts that make a difference. You can even show a stranger you care. Also on this day I could see that a lady who had alighted from the train had a lot to carry, her coat was being dragged, so I made her aware of this and she too was grateful.

I had cared for people in the community too, just to check to see if an old lady was all right and if she needed any groceries or to make a neighbour a cup of tea, or even just to offer someone your time with a listening ear.

Faith had actually said I could be an Earth Angel. As quickly as she had mentioned this, just as quickly I laughed it off saying, "What a kind remark." I was humbled.

After this short visit I was becoming breathless and informed the other ladies that I needed a sit down and a drink. There were few customers in the shop as it was not a particularly warm day.

We made our way across to the coffee shop. As the three of us sat in the window of the coffee shop, I closed my eyes and faced the sun. I started to ask the angels to help me. I felt terribly drained. I was urgently searching for my crystals in my pocket. I was in desperate need for their natural, powerful energies. I needed to hold them and meditate for a couple of minutes. In my mind I distanced myself from my surroundings, leaving the two ladies to talk amongst themselves.

As my eyes were closed and the sun was shining on me I saw Mother Mary in her blue gown holding baby Jesus. He was lit in a glow of pure white. The image stayed with me for a good few minutes. I instantly felt calm. On opening my eyes a few minutes later I saw both women still engaged in conversation.

Soon after, Faith had phoned to tell me she had come across a book on Earth Angels, it was the last one and she wondered if I was interested. I had just enough money and the urge was there to buy this book so we collected it as it was just across from where we were.

On our drive back I sat in the car reading about earth angels and their characteristics. I interrupted the other two in the front of the car to tell them that this book resembled my life. I read out snippets of the book. It even mentioned all my illnesses in this small book. At that moment in time I really felt the book was about my life.

Arriving home, Sharon, my eldest daughter, and I sat reading more of this book. Sharon had become tearful listening to me read. I must admit I too had become tearful as I felt my life was being reflected from the very pages I was reading.

✿✿✿

Intuitions are hunches, the feelings and the knowing that the information is accurate. Now I was starting to use my intuition, my urges were strong as I became more aware of them. These urges would get me through life.

I had now taken time to heal a lot of my family and whilst healing each of them I was feeling their symptoms. The symptoms were from fluttering in the chest to headaches, muscle pains, joint pain and anxiety. The symptoms were relieved sometimes for short periods and some miraculously disappeared altogether. The family members also informed me that they saw beautiful colours, angels and fairies while receiving healing.

✿✿✿

At this time I had also started explaining to my family to bear with me as I was going through a lot of changes. Where were these spiritual changes going to take me? I had no idea at this time.

Message for Sam

In the night I had two messages from a man who had passed over to the spirit world. I had never met him before and there he was standing in my bedroom. A short distance away from him was a little girl of about eight and opposite them was Sam, my neighbour. I could see this image whether my eyes were closed or open. I rubbed my eyes as I couldn't believe what I was seeing. Instantly I wrote the message down on a piece of paper that I had by my bedside. I glanced at the digital clock it was 00:54. The message was 'tell Sam everything is OK.' He repeated the message. My intuition was telling me she was not to worry. An hour later he came to me again. I saw exactly the same and yet again made another note.

Seeing is Believing

First of all I have to mention the time 00:54 the numbers add to 9, 9 divided by 3 equals 3. Three is The Trinity to Divine Truth. Firstly, the truth is given to me to pass on. The message was to be given to Sam as it was important. Maybe she had been worrying about the deceased man.

Secondly, I need to mention that Sam had twins and Jenna was one of the twins. She had passed over to the spirit world too, soon after she was born. Could this little girl have been Jenna?

Later in the night I had visions of the smoke detectors not working in the house, I could also hear them bleeping.

The next morning I asked if anyone else in the house had heard the smoke detectors bleeping the previous night but everyone was oblivious to it. Daren agreed the battery needed changing and did just that.

Sam arrived with her daughter Georgia at the front door. She wanted to speak to me about something before she set off for work. I also had the message from the night before written and folded in the palm of my hand.

Sam started telling me of her strange dream. In the dream she had come round for healing, which was a weird experience itself, she said it was like nothing she had experienced before. Then she went on to say that Rob, her deceased partner, had visited her in the dream at four o'clock. He said to her 'don't worry everything is going to be OK.' Sam looked at me confused as she said it was only a dream but seemed real. After she had finished telling me, I told her I had something to pass on to her. Frowning, she looked at me as I passed her the paper. She unfolded the paper and read the words. I explained how Rob had come to me twice at different times. Sam's mouth dropped open and she held out her hands, waiting for a further advance to this bizarre happening. We both stood at the door laughing nervously. As I calmed down, I could see the shock on Sam's face. She left the house spooked, screaming and waving her arms as she ran down the drive. I knew this was an important message from Rob.

Believing is Seeing

✿ ✿ ✿

As my spiritual awareness grew, I noticed how I was being drained by negative people and situations. Avoiding these situations and people was difficult as among them were my friends and family.

Added Pain

Sharon was having her theory driving test and was quite nervous. She required healing and soon after it she felt confident. I had absorbed her panic and was in need of a relaxant herbal remedy. I kept the remedy close by to calm myself when required. As we arrived at the test centre Sharon was sent to cubicle 9 and I instantly had faith she would do well. I made a point of sitting in the third chair in the waiting room for extra luck. Guess what? She passed, 100%.

✿ ✿ ✿

I had contacted Wei Ling, an ex-colleague and friend, to catch up on things as we had not spoken for a while. She came in and sat in one of the chairs in my conservatory. As we started talking I felt a terrible pain in my back. I knew this pain did not come from me. I certainly did not have it prior to her visit with me. As soon as I started asking her if she had pain in her back she said she did, although was not sure whether to say anything or not. The pain disappeared when she came in and sat down. However I did suffer with her pain for five days as well as my own.

The fibromyalgia pain was intense in my joints and muscles, the extra back pain, located to the top right belonged to Wei Ling.

Wei Ling asked me to help a friend of hers as she snored and did not like this when her boyfriend stayed over with her. So I felt that the healing would be acceptable and sent it to her friend in Manchester.

Apparently, when Wei Ling spoke to her friend, she found out the healing had actually been successful as her boyfriend informed her that she no longer snored. The feedback was interesting as I was told to keep up the good work.

Healing

I had also done some healing on a throat cancer patient as she was in desperate need. She had already had therapy on the cancer. As I could empathise and did not like to see others suffer I was willing to do what I could. Initially she asked for healing for her painful ear and throat. The healing was great. I felt confident that a significant change had been made for this lady. Her throat was very painful as I could sense the pain but the angels asked me to persevere. The pain subsided during the first ten minutes. Then I could see a desk with a piece of paper on it, a filing cabinet and stacks and stacks of boxes. After the session I gave her some feedback. She looked surprised and listened attentively. Soon after, she explained it was her work place that I could see. I think at this point I surprised myself.

✿ ✿ ✿

I had become quite interested in healing and offered healing to Paula.

During this session I was amazed to see a brain very clearly. I could see the cerebrum compact, just like you would see in a school text book. It was amazing. I knew why I was shown the brain, there was healing to be done in this area.

Throughout the healing process it was possible for me to see objects and people on the earthly planes, as well as from the spirit world. During this time it was not just the person's physiological being I was shown. The person receiving the healing would be relaxed as the healing energies entered the relevant areas in the body and the correct amount would be passed on through to them.

✿ ✿ ✿

Daren's mother had arthritic pain in her right hand. She sat in my conservatory complaining how she could not pick up objects and winced with pain. I offered her healing and she was open-minded about it, or faith healing as she called it. This seventy-five year old lady hardly ever complained about aches and pains but today was only too eager to show me the swelling in her right hand. She was quite relaxed throughout this session and afterwards we shared some information about how she found my hands very hot, she said it reminded her of being in Australia. As we sat talking she commented on her hand feeling flexible, it was quite amazing to see this and the swelling had gone down. She then sat at the dining room table for over half an hour writing with Tristen.

I truly do believe Angelic Reiki Healing is powerful and the healing goes to the most needed place in the body, mind and spirit.

I must admit, the healing had drained me and I was exhausted that night. My blurred grey vision returned with the pain.

Appointment with the Therapist

My friend Alison had taken me to see a practitioner for Aura-Soma® products as these were recommended by Rosemary. The practitioner lived on North Drive, I was quite surprised as the word 'north' was what I saw in my night vision whilst I was on the healing course. The number 12 was one of the products I had bought from the gentleman. Another vision comes true? The practitioner had commented I was wearing Aura-Soma Christ colours, which was fantastic as I resonate with Jesus Christ. At that moment I felt very happy as others were noticing my connection with Jesus Christ too.

Seeing is Believing

✿ ✿ ✿

I knew I had to make myself stronger physically, as much as my body would allow me. So I attended for my regular physiotherapy. I felt my therapist, Andrew, would not understand anything about spirituality, however he amazed me. He asked how I really felt and I informed him my spirits were high but felt that he would not understand if I told him more as he was a professional and a male. I had apologised for being sexist, but felt justified with this opinion as all the men I had told so far had just laughed at me.

He was enthusiastic and listened attentively. He remarked that he had been a physiotherapist for twenty years and not met anyone like me. I initially thought he was referring to me as an alien then he explained how he intuitively knew I was different from the many patients he had worked with. He complimented me on having this rare gift and wished me well with where ever it led me. This was an exciting day as I felt someone had truly understood me and where my compassion for helping people lay.

✿ ✿ ✿

Talking about spirituality enlightened people I knew, I was giving hope and understanding to them.

I also understand there are plenty of sceptics out there. Some of my own family are sceptics and only see things as black or white. I suppose it goes back to the saying 'seeing is believing.' Well I can certainly vouch that I do see and I do believe.

Beginning To Sort Out My Life

My oracle cards guided me to sort my life out and to take direction towards spiritual fulfilment. I was also being told that I needed to find deliverance from a traumatic situation. I could relate this to my sister's death seventeen and a half years ago. I knew I had to put things to rest properly to be able to move on. I did this through the help of the angels in meditation. My cards were relaying the same message of magical opportunities with self employment. Having had a small business was hard work but I had job satisfaction. At this moment in time I had no idea what would happen in the future.

Synchronistic Event

At my sister's house-warming party the children played happily whilst the adults greeted each other then indulged in fine food and drink. I now met more earth angels. There were 3 of us at this small affair. I was really happy as we discussed how each of us dealt with everyday life. As my brother-in-law and Daren joked about me seeing angels and feeling their presence, my sister's father-in-law just happened to join us and started telling us about his holidays abroad. He went on to say he used to see dead bodies from wars, hundreds of years ago. We all looked amazed at what he was telling us. I smiled and knew at that instance he was sent to say what he did so that the other two could reflect and realise that it was not just me who could see things. This synchronistic event was taking place for a reason. I was grateful for this gentleman's input, he was obviously clairvoyant.

Intuition

I had a mobile hairdresser whom I had known for a couple of years. She came regularly to cut the family's hair. She was a big lady with a warm personality. She was always concerned about me as I was breathless and fatigued each time she came. This particular day, she stood behind me cutting my hair. As I closed my eyes to rest them I could see her outline, as well as the problem in her stomach. I felt pain emanating from her back.

Seeing is Believing

I was now challenged by my own intuition to mention this to the hairdresser without upsetting her. As I was intuitively guided I addressed the issue. She admitted not being able to eat properly just lately. I offered her healing which she appreciated but I also informed her that more was required as the angels did not want me to finish so soon. She was keen and therefore agreed to have another session.

Seeing Anna

It was approaching autumn as the leaves were starting to fall off the trees but the weather was still quite pleasant as my daughter Alysha and I walked to the school at the top of my small road. Bob, our neighbour from the top end of the road had seen me walk past and kindly invited me in for a cup of tea.

I wanted to speak to Bob anyway, ever since his wife, Anna, had passed away almost six months ago, I felt I needed to tell him how much I wished I could have helped Anna. As much as I was concerned about Anna and her cancer returning she was just as much concerned for me as she saw me struggling. We used to talk on the phone occasionally and she was always full of good advice to keep me feeling well. I was quite distraught when I found out she had passed away even though I had not known her all that long.

Bob had gone into the kitchen to make me a cup of tea as I walked around the living room looking at Anna's photographs. There was a great chill in the room. Even though I had my coat on I felt the cold shivers run down my body. After looking at the photographs I sat on the sofa where I would normally sit when visiting Anna. Anna's chair was near the window. Every time we used to walk by she would always wave. I was quite sad to be in the house and felt the emotions in my throat. I struggled to swallow and a couple of tears flooded my eyes. Sitting there I saw a vibrational fuzz exactly where Anna would have sat. I was in awe of what I could see. Rubbing my eyes I could still see the fuzzy shape of Anna.

Believing is Seeing

Hoping she would touch me I held my hand out. At this time I was talking to Anna in my mind, telling her I knew she was there.

A few seconds later Bob walked in with my herbal tea. He sat on the other two seater sofa. I had already seen the tears in his eyes, aware that he was a very sensitive individual. Knowing this I did not want to upset him too much but knew I had to tell him what I saw and that it was still there. So I asked Bob if he had ever seen Anna or felt her presence in the bungalow. He shook his head to say he had not. I went on to tell him that Anna was in the same room as us, sitting in her chair. He took it quite well, shedding just a few tears. Within the next couple of minutes I could no longer see this fuzz. Looking over at Bob he sat with his arm over the back rest of the sofa and next to him I could see a white glow almost like an aura. I informed him Anna was now sitting next to him. At this stage he was very calm and collected as we chatted for a while. My intuition told me he would benefit from healing, which I offered to him. He seemed interested in trying it at some point.

Chapter Five

Oracle Cards

I had been feeling special as these events in my daily life were taking place. I started to wonder why this was happening to me and I felt overwhelmingly honoured. I knew I could help people, but to what extent?

My oracle cards were now informing me how I needed to set my sights higher and find something lost from life, also to nourish body, mind and spirit and work towards spiritual fulfilment.

It was strange, but I appreciated how I had my husband, children and neighbours supporting me. Without my children helping to cook and clean and to do things for me I just do not know where I would be. There was guilt that they were doing this but I was also encouraged to gain my health back as I was so desperate to move on from the debilitating health condition.

✪ ✪ ✪

People I knew were now having their cards read and amazingly they were true to their lives, and for some the cards were coming out the same each time when changes were not made or situations had not been addressed.

I visited a friend of mine who had had a knee operation. Arriving at Dianne's home, I found that she had family visiting too, they had travelled a long distance. They knew I had my cards with me and became interested in having a reading. Before I knew it there was a queue of people. Sitting in her large kitchen at the table I read each person's cards in turn, finding that some things revealed were relevant to their lives.

That night I had a message for Dianne's sister who was a nurse. The message was from the angels. I could clearly see an open book and in the top left hand corner was a hand written message. The words were 'there is a message.' Straight after this a spirit was trying to make contact but I did not know who.

The following morning I contacted Dianne and spoke to her sister. Initially, I passed on the message and then asked her if someone close to her had recently passed away. I told her it was not a family member. Instantly she said her close friend passed to the spirit world just three weeks ago. I told her that the deceased person was trying to make contact and the angels wanted her to know there was a relevant message for her in a book.

I had left this lady with the information. At that point I knew I had done my duty.

Jayne arrived with her twenty one year old son, Daren, as he was interested in a card reading. His cards were read in private and he was a little surprised to see the similar cards come out from each pack. I liked to keep a variety of packs so that the person having the reading could select a pack or I would select one intuitively. Daren has had some strange experiences in his life which he did not quite know the reasons why. After chatting with him and Jayne, I felt that they now had some answers to the mysterious happenings he had encountered.

I was hoping to go back to my cultural work I did with children when I recovered. But looking for an answer the cards were guiding me to find deliverance from a situation and allow closure to break free. Did this mean what I was thinking? Was I really never to work in the field I enjoyed?

Seeing is Believing

Kevin

As I was trying to get in touch with my brother-in-law Kevin by telephone, he suddenly appeared at my backdoor. He was very sceptical about my healing and experiences that I had been having. As we sat in the conservatory, I suddenly picked up a headache which I knew was not mine. No one else in the room admitted it was them who had a headache. Kevin decided he would have some healing but would not tell me where his aches and pains were. I went with the flow of the healing and found the pain that he had and saw his deceased wife whilst healing. He was surprised by the findings. Not to mention that the headache was Kevin's. He left laughing. I think he was just testing me!

The Guardian Angel

Tristen had been standing at the top of the stairs this particular evening when he saw a person with dark hair and a white gown follow Sharon into the living room. He quickly ran down the stairs to find Sharon was sitting on her own, flicking through a magazine. He then asked her if she had walked in by herself. She looked at him quizzically and replied of course. Then he told her what he had seen. Sharon did not seem to be too bothered but Tristen came running to tell me. I was shocked to hear this and listened intently as he described the height and appearance of this being. I intuitively knew he had seen her guardian angel. Coincidently Sharon had been asking for the name of her guardian angel that day.

I was now aware that Tristen was clairvoyant.

A few days later Sharon asked her guardian angel if she was going to pass her driving test as it was not too far ahead. That same day she found a white feather on her car. That happened in a space of two hours as it was not there when we were at home. This gave her hope as she was obviously very excited and felt very confident at the prospect of driving her own car.

Past Life Healing

With the training of Angelic Reiki we also received past life healing methods. It is believed that we carry our many past life traumas, physical and emotional pains with us into the present life.

Sharon indicated an interest in this and then we started the healing. The past lives were in motion. It was like being in a movie. During the first part of that session I saw Sharon running and it seemed like a big mammal was chasing her. A dinosaur was what I could see and then a monkey appeared and it hid in the bushes.

In the second part I could see a person with a bob haircut running around in what appeared to be a cave.

Finally, in the last part of the healing session I saw a pirate with a skull and cross bones flag. During this session Sharon felt pain in various parts of her body, though she did say it was a bearable experience. Sharon could also see fairies and someone sitting in front of her, in her mind's eye. She became emotional as the loving presence she felt overwhelmed her.

Back to See Dorothea

Going back to see Dorothea, the healer, was exciting. We sat in her dining room allowing the natural daylight to shine in on us through her patio doors. She told me that my psychic powers were developing and to look out for messages on the bathroom mirror with the steam. I listened to what she said but did not pay too much attention to it.

We carried on chatting and then Dorothea offered to read my cards for me. Well blow me down, the cards were fantastic and more to the point, my spiritual journey was yet to blossom! It was strange because I already knew most of the information the cards were telling me. I liked Dorothea because she had a lovely genuine character. She spoke from her heart with the help from her spirit guides illuminating her powers and energies. Feeling comfortable with her we chatted further about my life and everything began to make much more sense.

Before leaving, I reminded Dorothea about going to see Gordon Smith, a barber who has psychic powers. There were a few people interested in going to see him and as the time grew nearer I was looking forward to seeing him myself.

I had been told I was psychic but not by any means to the level of these people on stage. I was intrigued to hear his stories.

Words of Encouragement

By now some friends were becoming interested in my experiences and came to listen to more of my stories. I was now becoming more intuitive and could pick up energies from people I was talking to. Some were unhappy in their work place, some were lost in life and some were just floating in the ocean, allowing the waves to take them adrift. My words of encouragement flowed almost like a counsellor's. My friends thanked me in return although I felt I was not making a huge difference to their lives but they felt I was helping.

✿ ✿ ✿

When Wei Ling came for a healing session she seemed quite excited as she did not know what to expect. The room was pleasantly warm and there was still daylight on that early October afternoon. After our chat we proceeded with the healing. She relaxed in the chair in the conservatory with the angelic music playing in the background.

Believing is Seeing

As I finished the healing I could see tears running down Wei Ling's cheeks. Handing over some tissues to her, she smiled and said she was fine. I thought perhaps this was an overwhelming experience for her just like it was for Sharon.

Wei Ling had no idea where the tears had come from as she said it was strange because they had not fallen from her eyes. Yet visibly they were there. She could not understand this as she had not felt overly emotional. The tears were flowing for some reason and I believe it was the love she felt as she also sensed some enveloping of wings. This lady was fine and left cheerfully.

✿ ✿ ✿

I was still not feeling entirely well and still having physiotherapy on a weekly basis, wondering when I was to be in good health. Maybe I just needed to say my daily affirmations of good health that Dorothea gave me? I felt that it could contribute to my well-being.

The Man on the Stall

Paula had told me about a market stall close to where I lived. After my physiotherapy appointment I thought I would make a visit. It was a cold wet, day but I was intrigued to see what he was selling. The man on the stall had recognised me from the 'Second Sight' evening with the authors. He commented how well I had spoken that evening, lifting the sombre mood. I was grateful for his comments whilst looking at his goods for sale. We chatted for a while as he told me he was going to see Gordon Smith too. For some reason I was very comfortable in that man's presence. After leaving the stall I went into St. Mary's Church which was nearby. I felt I needed a few minutes in this holy building. I felt calm and at peace as I looked at the glass stained windows and the sculpted statue of Jesus Christ.

Seeing is Believing

When I returned home coincidently Marlene and I sat watching Gordon Smith on the television, who we were to see in a few days.

Meeting Colleagues

Lyn, Caroline and I had arranged a date to meet at the angel shop, some miles away. The weather was particularly bad as there was a lot of rain. The mist was spraying off the lorries and vehicles. As I was driving there I became more and more exhausted with increasing breathing difficulties. I decided to ask my guardian angel and other healing angels to help me. I could not believe it, within minutes I could feel a cushioning all around me, especially my head. My ears were enveloped, I knew instantly the angels were there, feeling very safe and guarded. I thanked them for their help in getting me safely to my destination.

I met Lyn in the angel shop, we greeted with a hug and briefly chatted as we waited for Caroline. We were seemingly the first customers in the shop. I had asked the assistant to play a track from the compact disc that I was interested in buying. She played it as I wandered around the shop with Lyn, the music was very pleasant and soothing.

My mobile phone rang and when I answered it a voice said, "Hello I am phoning from 'Angels Bring Love' to let you know that the fairy cards you had ordered have arrived." I glanced at Lyn with a frown on my face and then made my way to the middle of the aisle facing the lady in the shop as she was holding the phone. I said to her "Oh, OK, that's fine did you want me?" pointing to myself. She watched me walk over and the pair of us were still clutching the telephones. She then looked at me surprised, and even said 'yes' and 'goodbye' before she put the telephone down. Well surprisingly, this had happened a couple of times before in that very shop. We stared in amazement. It was funny. We giggled and agreed it was a coincidence. She said she did look at me as she dialled the number for some strange reason, but denied her intuition that it was me she was trying to contact.

Caroline had now arrived and so we set off to Lyn's house to catch up on how we had all got on since we last met. Lyn welcomed us into her tranquil home. We had a cup of herbal tea and relaxed into conversation. Not long after I was feeling depleted of energy and breathless. At that time I did wonder how I was going to get back home.

We decided to do some healing on one another. The healing that Caroline and Lyn had done on me was strange as I actually felt as if something had been removed from my stomach. I could feel myself now not as breathless as before. I appreciated the healing that was given to me.

It was a much needed gathering as we are all 'on the same wave length,' as I like to call it. We had arranged to meet regularly which we all thought was important for us.

When I returned home I could not wait to try out my new oracle cards. They revealed that I had risen above problems in my past and now I needed to honour my true feelings as I will start to feel safe in the future.

Meeting Jacqueline

Alysha had wanted to see Jacqueline Wilson, the children's author. The queue was never ending and it was rather tiring for me. As I needed to sit down, I sat on the steps leading up to where the author was signing her books. We had taken part in the author's competition. We were unsure of some answers to the questions and guessed them. However we both commented that we most probably would not win, looking at each other doubtfully.

Alysha was overjoyed meeting Jacqueline whilst Daren took a photograph to put in a keepsake album.

Receiving a phone call from the bookstore to say that Alysha had won a runner up prize for the Jacqueline Wilson competition was fantastic as my children do not normally win competitions. As soon as I had put the telephone down I screamed with joy for my daughter. For all the people that must have taken part and we had guessed the answers, to win was very good. That day we collected the prize Alysha was over the moon to say the least and could not wait to show her friends at school.

I do believe this was unusual and still we had a bit of help from somewhere.

Pain in the Foot

Alison, my friend, had called round with her children because her mother had sent an 'Angel of Faith' for me, for healing her throat. It was a beautiful gesture and received graciously.

Alison had been limping whilst in my house. She was complaining about struggling for days and felt something could be injured in her foot as she had banged it on a concrete slab in her garden. As we discussed this pain I immediately had pain and cramp in my foot, it was the same foot and location as hers. I did not know if Alison had noticed this. With a strange feeling inside, I sat there massaging my foot, gritting my teeth. It took some time, then, slowly the pain eased off. Alison walked out of my house with no pain and texted me by mobile phone to tell me that amazingly her foot was fine.

✿ ✿ ✿

On a wet Monday morning my hairdresser returned for some more healing. We sat in the conservatory admiring some beautiful hair designs in the magazine. As time was ticking away and she was a busy lady, we went into the Angelic Reiki session. During the healing I could see she had problematic ovaries, as well as other minor symptoms such as pain in her right foot and pain in her head. During feedback I mentioned female problems. The lady said she had not menstruated for seven years. I was surprised as I had not heard of this before. It was obviously a medical condition that her doctor was aware of. She was also desperate to try and lose a bit of weight which I did ask for assistance from the angels to give this lady the will power to achieve this. We will have to wait and see if she can be helped with her weight problem, I do believe regular treatments are needed for long standing problems. However she did leave a lot calmer than she arrived.

Still in autumn, I really enjoyed soaking in the sun, breathing in the fresh air and watching the clouds pass by. I have learned to appreciate everything around me. It is Natures' beauty that we take for granted. Ill health has dawned upon me to make me see and realise what truly is beautiful. I am very grateful and appreciate this world I live in.

Chapter Six

Seeing Gordon Smith

I looked forward to being in a social atmosphere as I had not done this in a while. The four of us met at a theatre to see Gordon Smith. Silly me, I had left the tickets at home and time was running out to go back and get them. Luck had it that Marlene's partner Mike was available to bring them to us.

We guessed Gordon Smith was there to promote his new book but more interestingly still we wanted to see what he was all about. I met Dorothea by chance with her friends as we were about to enter and we spoke briefly.

As we waited for Gordon to arrive on stage the theatre was filling up. The man from the angel store was there too, sitting on front row.

Gordon had started his talk about spirits and his psychic abilities. I was flabbergasted to see things lifting from his body.

As he stood in front of the red velvet curtains there appeared to be spirits leaving him via his crown chakra. This was a little more than startling to me. When I asked the other three ladies if they could see the same they replied they could not. That evening was however interesting and as we were leaving we met Dorothea again and she did actually say she did see what I saw and more. I felt I was not on my own.

A Busy Night

Well during the night, I had a wonderful experience. It started at 12:05am when I saw a shield with a phoenix and lots of symbols. I could not remember which symbols they were because they flashed before my eyes and there were so many of them. My intuition told me that Archangel Michael was keeping me safe and protected with his shield. The phoenix was showing me that there would be transformations I was to undergo at this present time. I believe I received some symbols from the hierarchy of angels for my future service. At this stage I was unsure of what that would be.

For some reason Archangel Michael and Archangel Raphael were present and worked on my physical body. I could feel the physical pain in my lungs and stomach. The angels were surrounding me. I could see their wings, it was an experience I could not put into words and it lasted an hour. After that I felt the sensation of each chakra opening and some sort of work being done on each one of them, starting from the crown. During this time I felt a waft of air on my face yet everything was still around me. For the rest of the night I could see spirit orbs of white floating around the room and shadows of spirits just wandering. Well, what a busy night!

The unusual clanging of thunder and bolts of lightning woke me up the next morning. As I pondered on the goings on from the previous night, I remembered seeing 11 in the mist of the bathroom window the day before. The date was 11th October when all the angels were working on me!

Past Life Healing

Alison L. one of my friends, had arranged with me to do some past life healing. She was intrigued and wanted to release any imbalances in her life.

We started the healing once she was comfortable. By closing our eyes and feeling a sense of calm, I took us away from the surroundings. Soon after, appearing in front of me were lots of flashes that I could not understand. I asked the angels what it was. Then the images become clearer. It was a beautiful sun with slight traces of clouds. I just knew it was not British weather, it was in another country but where I did not know at that moment. An animal ran past, it was a deer. I could then see a big round bump, it was a pregnant lady. It was Alison. Nearby this lady was a tepee with a fixed flap as a doorway, I could just make out the stitching on it. I then felt pain in my left arm and a sensation of dragging. What I could see was that Alison was a Native American lady. The whole tribe had been taken over by another tribe. They were all being pulled by an attachment of rope in a line. After a while I felt terrible pain in my stomach and a sharp stabbing pain in my side. As this had happened, Alison's head kept drooping down. I checked to see if she was all right. Then I felt energies being drained from my body. By now Alison's head had dropped further down. The healing had come to an end therefore, I closed all past life healing. Then Alison and I were back in our surroundings.

As we discussed what was revealed she said she felt jerks in her body and her head kept drooping. She struggled to push her head back. In her life as a Native American lady she was captured and tortured when eventually her life came to an abrupt end. She was intrigued and surprised by her past life experience.

Moved By Blessings

One morning I looked out of the bedroom window and just happened to notice that the angel blessings had moved again. They were put in a clump on the window sill. And now they were in two rows facing north again. I asked the family if anyone had done this as I still liked to make sure if anyone had moved them. Nobody in the house had done so. Sharon said she had found them like that when she came in from college and I was out of the house for my hospital appointment.

Blessings moved north

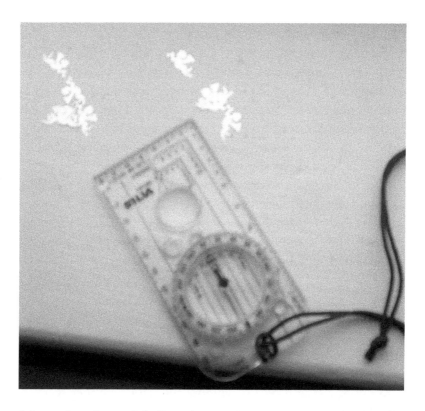

After a few days of feeling sharp pains in my chest just like the previous winter I became worried as I did not want to go through pleurisy pains again, so I booked myself in for a flu vaccination, but I had a 3 week wait.

Due to the wait of my flu jab, Lyn had recommended a healer she knew. I knew I had to do something else to prevent the pains and to make myself feel better. I had booked to see this young man and was looking forward to my first healing session with him. In the mean time I asked Lyn and Caroline if they could send me some distant healing as I was struggling.

Feeling Fragile

I gingerly moved around the house as I felt very fragile again.

I had my sister's house-warming the next day but felt too unwell to travel. So I consulted my oracle cards. Remarkably the same card came out 3 times. It was the brother's and sister's card and that was a sure enough answer that I should be there.

During the night I felt the pains had minimised somewhat as Lyn had sent healing and I had done some myself. Caroline also sent distant healing and told me of the problems in my solar plexus and heart centre, there was a cluster of bells on each and a laughing Buddha. This made sense to me as it was a clearing and cleansing process. The Buddha and the bells were a clearing and cleansing my energy centres. When there are blockages in the chakras illness can occur.

I had taken my time to get myself ready as my energies were very low. Feeling fragile I needed to heal myself while Daren drove seventy miles to where my sister lived.

Meeting the family and enjoying being in company was good for me. However there were family members there who despised me for the way I coped with my challenges in life. Because of the decisions I had made in my life they did not agree with them. Therefore, they saw me as the black sheep of the family and told me I had no connections with them. This hurt me a lot. But I was only too wary myself and kept my distance after being told this. From here on there was no relationship and I had tried in the past to get along. Perhaps they could not accept and see the light in a person. Perhaps they too wished they too could break free and be their own person.

✿ ✿ ✿

Talking about angels touched the hearts of those who believed. My sister's mother-in-law, Erna, also had a lovely angelic experience and before departing she gave me her fairy broach. It was truly

69

beautiful. I was happy and taken aback that she had given me something that belonged to her.

My energies were drained regularly as I tried to get up to do things for myself. I have never been a lazy person, and being unable to do things was very frustrating. Sometimes I was just paralysed for a couple of hours unable to move, not even able to move my finger. I could not even speak and could only see grey. It was as though my body wanted to shut down. Daren had come home a few times to find half of my body on the sofa and half on the floor or slumped, with tears rolling down my face. I was never going to just give up. I just needed to wait for it to pass. He made me comfortable until my energies were boosted and even then I had to be very careful.

Not Meant to Be

My neighbour Marlene had borrowed the film based upon the book, *The Da Vinci Code* from her son, so we could watch it at my house. We were excited at this much talked about film. When we had made ourselves comfortable and sat with a cup of tea to watch the film, it was playing but it kept on jerking. I had a lot of pain in my heart centre, it was a crushing sensation and I tried to massage this area, which was not being relieved. Marlene's son had watched it only the night before so there should have been no problem with it. After numerous times of stopping and playing the film we decided that it could play better at Marlene's house. Marlene lived across the road so we toddled along. Marlene inserted the film into the player and yet again the film did not play properly. When she removed the film from the player she found a large scratch on it covering the entire disc. My intuition was telling me not to watch the film even though I was intrigued. Eventually we did watch the film. After watching it we noticed something else had moved in the house.

Seeing is Believing

Alysha had collected some natural stones from the beach from our holiday. She had put them in a pile on my bedroom windowsill. We woke to find they were put in a mirror image pyramid shape. Instantly this reminded me of the film we watched. The same shape is in the film itself. As above so below, pyramid. Although, I have not one hundred percent put my finger on the reason why the stones were placed in pyramid shapes, I do believe the meaning is that what is created above can be created on earth.

Returning home I went to the toilet upstairs. As I walked out of the bathroom, I saw a small white misty glow coming up the stairs from the corner of my eye. Wow! I knew there was definitely something there, was this the little girl who followed me around? It will all make sense a little later, so please read on.

✿✿✿

Alison L and Shaun had invited Daren and me to their house for a meal. Daren was now a vegetarian and Alison had cooked two meals. I had the meat dish with a glass of wine. As much as I was looking forward to the meal I felt I could not eat all the meat. That night I felt rather unwell. I told Daren that I was being told not to drink even the occasional social beverage and to give up the meat. Also that night, I was given more symbols. It was great to see the symbols but I was consciously unaware of their spiritual meaning. They appeared at the time quite clearly but as they came so fast and many of them I am unable to elaborate on them.

Chapter Seven

The Young Healer

I had twisted my pelvis as I got ready for my visit to see the healer. I hoped this would not cause me too many problems driving, although it was an uncomfortable journey. I had asked the angels to help me get to the area where he lived. Where this gentleman lived made sense, it was an appropriate name place I thought for a light worker. A lightworker is a person who is committed to Divine service for the highest good of others.

I arrived there without any trouble considering I was not too confident in finding places. I remembered to thank the angels for their support.

As I knocked on the door I was surprised to see a very young looking man opening the door. Standing there he looked more like sixteen years of age. After the greeting he took me up to the healing room. On the landing was some beautiful art work. I could relate to the large oil paintings as I had those images in my minds eye and when I heal. As I admired the paintings he told me he was the artist. Well, I thought he was very talented.

We chatted about my health and then he started the healing. He was very busy working on me. I could feel the surges of energy flow through. I thought I heard voices, but they were not clear enough for me to understand what was said. I was aware that spiritual people can hear voices. After the healing we talked. He said he could feel my lung problems and had sensations in his body indicating the areas where my problems lay spiritually within my body.

This was interesting as my throat was one of the problems. I was told I do not express myself.

This was correct as I was always very quiet as a child, the little girl sitting at the back of the classroom. The one the teachers never knew existed, almost invisible. Looking back at all of my school reports I can honestly say it was repeatedly said that I was very quiet.

Seeing is Believing

Growing up I had been pushed around in the wide ocean like a piece of driftwood, unable to set my own course. At times I was brave enough to make my own decisions.

Spiritually my lungs had been suppressed as I had not been able to breathe my own breath. I was breathing in others breath to please them. I spoke to please others. I did things to please others.

As I was being told information about myself I had a lump in my throat, my emotions were ready to spill out just like an overflowing sink of water. I swallowed deeply and pushed my emotions down, leaving just a twinkle of tear in my eye. He continued telling me more.

The young man could actually see Alysha's face and he told me she looked angelic. Well that was true because she does. He told me she had a star on her forehead. I did not know what he meant by this, I guessed he meant spiritually. He also told me that not only was I clairvoyant, so were two of my children. He told me Alysha was scared of seeing and being on her own. This was very true as she would only stay in a room of people: even Paula had noticed it when she came to visit just a few days previously. Alysha had become scared and more sensitive since my channels had opened. I told him that I had tried to explain there was nothing to be frightened of and that I would not let anything happen to her.

At that interesting meeting with the healer he had told me a lot of things which amazed me. How could he know so much at such a young age? He was of course an old and wise soul who received help from his spirit guide.

It was a good journey back home. I had a feeling of well-being and elated to meet such a gifted person.

When I got home I brushed Alysha's hair aside to reveal a chickenpox scar exactly in the centre of her third eye shaped in a star. I called Sharon into the living room to show her what that young man had told me. She looked startled too.

That very evening Alysha told us she had an imaginary friend. Sitting at the dinner table whilst tucking into her pasta she told the family her name was Zoe and she was eleven years old. Sharon sat opposite to Alysha, gently she made conversation and asked what colour hair Zoe had. Alysha went on to describe her with brown curly long hair, telling us she was at the table too. So Daren jokingly stuck his tongue at where Alysha said she was sitting. Alysha made a point of telling Daren that Zoe had stuck her tongue out back to him. Eating his dinner, he chuckled.

Along with Daren, Tristen would not believe Alysha either, whereas Sharon and I were interested to hear more. Alysha informed us how Zoe liked fashion, it was a detailed description of her wardrobe. She described Zoe's bed clothes in such great detail that it had to be heard. Zoe had apparently left the room and Alysha waved at Zoe, her imaginary friend, watching her walk upstairs. Well I believed her as it appeared to be very real for Alysha even though we could not see Zoe.

As Alysha had followed Zoe upstairs without being scared, we did actually think back to just a couple of days earlier as she was now entering rooms without being scared.

When Alysha had come down stairs again we asked more about Zoe. She told us that Zoe slept in her bed, top to toe. They both did the homework giggling on the bed. She also said that Zoe went to school with her and told us where she sat in the classroom. Taking in all of this information we were told that she was no longer scared because Zoe was with her. I could not disregard what I was being told. I understood Alysha and just knew this was her guardian angel comforting her.

The Face of Christ

As I meditate often I think of Jesus Christ. In my healing sessions I also invoke Jesus to assist me.

That same evening, Tristen had stood at the kitchen sink and as he filled himself a glass of water he saw the face of Jesus Christ immediately in front of him. The image he saw awed him leaving him speechless for a few minutes. He then came running into the conservatory to tell me what he saw and yet again the detail was there. Jesus Christ's long hair, with a slim face calmly staring at him. Sitting there reading my book I was happy that he had seen the image. Without a doubt he did see.

Start of Aura Reading

On our way home by car from the bookstore Alysha had noticed a blue line on the wall in the rear view mirror. Let me explain, this line was not painted on the wall. The line was above the wall. It is the first layer that is seen by the eye when aura reading. Everywhere she looked the electric blue line was more obvious to the eye. Driving along she was pointing out more auras. When we got home Alysha pointed out to the rest of the family what she could see. As I was already aware of auras I could read them too. We could now read the same auras on people as well as objects.

Family Holiday

We had travelled with family to our holiday destination by the sea. What a fantastic view from our accommodation. The surfers were out daily in seven foot waves even in October. Whilst on the holiday I saw the faces of Saint Germain and Jesus Christ. The faces I could see were actually on Daren's t-shirt, they were not prints but folds in the t-shirt. This made me think back to months before attending the Angelic Reiki course that I had seen Djwal Khul and Saint Germain then.

They were appearing to me for some reason. Was it to encourage me to stay on the spiritual path?

On a day trip out by the sea, I took the opportunity to submerge my feet in the lapping sea waves. The sea was not as cold as I expected for the time of year. As I gazed into the distant ocean I thanked God for my healing and cleansing with the seawater. I could have stayed longer but needed a sit down. When we got ashore the others went to the top of the hill, while I sat on a rock enjoying the waves and the amazing view appreciating the natural and free things in life.

After retreating to the accommodation I needed to rest. As I closed my eyes I saw a gentleman who has passed to the spirit world. He gave a message for my mother-in-law.

When I get messages I feel it is my duty to pass them on. The messages could be from deceased loved ones or the angels.

Remembering my times of feeling unheard I now knew that I needed to stand my ground. Just as my cards had been telling me recently, I had done exactly that. I felt that standing my ground, resulted in seeing many lights, angel orbs flashing in my bedroom. I believe they were helping me through the situation. It was beautiful to see, as I calmly fell asleep.

During our time away from home we were all in turn complaining of nausea. On our last night away Tristen had been the one who felt quite ill. I decided to stay with him whilst the rest of the family went out. He lay on the sofa fast asleep with little energy. I lay nearby him and as I closed my eyes I saw the face of Christ. The image of Jesus was recurring in my closed eye view. A little later I did some healing for Tristen. When Daren came back to the accommodation Tristen sat up feeling quite well. His sickness had worn off while I was left feeling ill.

Angel in the Moon

The evening was beautiful and the moon was shining into the conservatory. The rest of the family were in the living room watching television. Sharon had requested healing which I was always ready to do, as she had her driving test very soon and she was quite anxious. I had started healing her but not long after I was inclined to close down the healing as her anxiety was a little too much for me. As we sat talking, looking up at the moonlit sky we both saw the perfect shape of a very slim angel in front of the moon. She was on a side view with one of her legs bent slightly higher than the other and her arms flowing behind her. We were awed by the sight. It was just like one I had seen before, she was perfectly amazing. I was pleased to have caught that scene and so was Sharon. Was the real reason to close down the healing so mother and daughter could both see the beautiful angel?

Dreaming

While dozing into a deep sleep, the dream had started.

I saw my friend Alison sitting on a chair, the place was quite spacious but I did not know where it was. Next to her was her baby in a pushchair. I was also there sat next to them holding another baby whom I assumed was Alison's too. As we sat talking she got up from her chair and walked towards a man with long dark brown hair. They chatted for a while as I watched both babies. When I glanced up at them they were kissing passionately. I was so embarrassed that I could no longer sit there looking at the pair. So I stood up and walked a few steps away with the baby still in my arms. After a few more minutes they were disagreeing about something and then the dream came to an abrupt end.

The dream was so clear and vivid I knew I had to tell Alison.

When I had retold the dream to her we both were in fits of laughter, for she was happily married with two children.

This dream will be explained a little later.

Negative Feeling

Sharon was about to have her first driving test and was ready for another dose of healing. After the healing we asked the oracle cards if she was to pass her test. No relevant cards were coming out. I did have a negative feeling. The dream from the previous night was of a person driving a red car like Sharon's but she was not driving it. I decided to use my crystal pendulum as this was another means of guidance and would give me an answer to my question. I asked the pendulum if she would pass her test that day: the answer was 'no.' Needless to say she failed her test and was quite distraught. After the initial breakdown and tears we booked another test.

The Little Girl

Tristen was on the landing passing unused items to his dad to put in the loft. As soon as everything was done he came down to find me sitting in the living room. As I glanced up he told me he was standing holding the ladder when he saw a little girl. She stood near him. I asked him what she looked like. He pulled his hand away from his pocket to estimate how high she was. He did this in a very calm manner considering he was telling me about something paranormal. Taking a guess the height was about two and a half feet. Tristen had said she was four years old with blonde hair.

I had never told the children what Dorothea had told me. Never mind about the little girl. For him to say she was four so confidently as if he already knew that was her age. The description was just like Dorothea had said, a blonde haired girl who tugged on my clothes. This was now intriguing, as Tristen told me that when he was bent over cleaning out the hamsters a few days earlier he had felt a tugging on his shirt but when he turned around to look no one was there!

Well that was three of us, sighting and sensing that little girl. The small misty glow on the stairs I had seen recently was her. I just know it. I do believe she really is here.

Days later, still unafraid and confident, Tristen spoke about seeing the blonde haired little girl in the living room. He said she stood near the plant in the corner of the room. However, he never spoke to her which I thought could be interesting. Would there be a reply? Has she got a specific message? Why is she with us?

Dream Come True ?

Alison and I had arranged to meet for a coffee at a garden centre which was only a couple of miles down the road. We sat and chatted as we drank our beverages. Amelie, the baby, became bored, wanting to get out of the baby chair. Alison was interested in a pet snake for her eldest daughter so she wanted to speak with the reptile keeper. I had offered to take hold of Amelie so that Alison could query about buying a snake, without running around after an infant. As I picked up Amelie and wandered a few feet away I turned around to find Alison talking to a man with long dark brown hair and I was holding the baby. I gasped, with my eyes nearly popping out of my head. As Alison looked round to see if I was coping with her baby, I stood puzzled and I pointed to the man. At this stage she did not know why I was making sign language. I put Amelie down to toddle for a few minutes and we made our way to her mother. As soon as they had finished talking I whispered to Alison, "Who were you talking to? Turn round and look." As she did so I reminded her of the man in my dream. Her mouth dropped open then we both shrieked with laughter, leaving the man staring at us, confused. Giggling we left the centre. Amazed by my dream, Alison told me it was all a bit strange and too close for comfort!

Chapter Eight

Going Back To See the Healer

Going back to see the young healer I got lost because I had not asked for help from the angels.

Finally, when I got there, he greeted me at the front door and I followed him up to the therapy room. Soon he started the healing and I found myself subconsciously drifting away from the room I was lying in. Losing sense of my surroundings I went into a deep state of relaxation. Whilst receiving the healing, I felt a sharp pain in my heart as if I had been stabbed. I also had pain in my sacro iliac joints. Other than that I felt relaxed. Becoming aware of my surroundings after the session I felt quite tired. The young man had told me where my connections lay in Egypt and India in past lives.

Well, I do believe that we have lived many lives before, so this was very fascinating to hear. The information that I was given, somewhat linked with my present life. The pain that I experienced during the healing in fact linked with the pain I had suffered only a few years ago. I went away fascinated and impressed by the man's talents and gift.

I was tired due to not having sufficient sleep the previous night.

Driving home on the long slip road, I realised I should have been on the dual carriageway. I was in the wrong lane!

It was a busy Friday afternoon during rush hour. I tried to get across to the correct lane without thinking how fast the traffic was flowing behind me and in the lane parallel to me. I made this dangerous move not realising it at that time.

As quickly as I moved across, something pulled the car back into the lane I was travelling in. Shocked by the sight of nearly causing a major accident I could see people in their vehicles cursing me.

My eyes filled with tears and I trembled, feeling both apologetic and ashamed.

The move was senseless. I could have been in a terrible dilemma. I should have driven on the slip road and rejoined the dual carriageway a little further.

All the way home I whimpered with shame. I was shaken up and in need of a cup of tea.

Drinking tea later in my living room, I sat thinking about this difficult situation.

Sitting there a memory came to me. Nine years ago, I was learning to drive. I was also heavily pregnant with my youngest child. I had a dream. The dream was about me driving a car on a dual carriageway. To the left of the carriageway was a brick wall. The car I was driving crashed into the wall.

As the car crashed in the dream, I woke up to reality breathless with a thud in my heart, and then my waters broke. I then gave birth to Alysha 4 ½ weeks early, resulting in a split pelvis or symphysis pubis dysfunction as I was told by a physiotherapist. The pelvic injury was a debilitating and chronically painful condition which left me disabled for almost four years.

This would be the same place where I nearly crashed my car driving home after seeing the healer. The area I veered away from, just in time, was where the slip road and the dual carriageway were about to meet near a brick wall. Exactly how I saw it all in the dream! This left me very emotional and in even more shock since the dream had almost become reality.

Moved By the Angel

I had now my own room, dedicated to the angels and many Ascended Masters. I had finished meditating and went upstairs to put something away. I looked over to the window to find the eleven inch angel that I had standing facing my bed had moved. This beautiful figure was now facing the door and then to see all the angel blessings placed perfectly around her was surprising to say the least! I stood looking at the door and then at the angel. I was receiving a clear message. It was telling me 'the door is open, walk through it, the angels are with you.' This was the door to my future. As usual I was overjoyed as this was yet more confirmation about my spiritual journey. My heart could not express how much love and acceptance I felt at that time. I was definitely moved by the angel. In fact it always took days for me to come down to earth as one would say.

Angelic Music

It was a week day and the children were getting ready for school. I had struggled to get myself dressed and presentable for the day so we were running late. Walking down the stairs I thought about doing two things, my morning cleansing ritual and putting my angelic music on. The aura cleansing prepared me for the day of self healing and meditation.

As I entered the kitchen I heard the first track playing on the player in the conservatory. No one was downstairs. The doors to the conservatory were closed but the music penetrated through to the kitchen even though the night before, I had watched Tristen switch the power off to the music system. Amazed yet again to see that no one had been in the conservatory I realised that a miracle had happened. The angels were determined to help me cleanse. I could not thank the angels enough for their support. Just as much as they helped me, the more I became dedicated to them.

Feeling Special

My weekly visit to see the young healer had soon arrived again. I looked forward to attending the session, although this time it was to have a card reading. The in-depth reading was telling me that I wanted to fly; I could do a lot more with my life. I had no idea how restricted I had become spiritually.

I know I can fly. I can do this through spiritual teachings and helping others. I already had a good idea of many things that were said to me. My intuition was telling me I was capable of helping others through my own experiences. It was just that knowing.

But some of the information was unbelievable. I was told I would hear a miracle voice. I took note of what was being said. Before the healer went on to speak about my mission on earth, I felt a glow of warmth wash over me and I had a feeling of knowing something special was waiting for me. I have felt special before now. We all have the right to feel special. We are all children of God. Many times I have questioned why I was in the body that I am. Who am I really? Have I been dropped off from another planet? Why are people so cruel? Even to this day I cannot believe that cruelty exists.

Dreaming Of a Girl

Retiring to bed that evening I had a vivid dream about a little girl. She had blonde hair and appeared very gaunt. I could see her looking over a car bonnet. It was in fact a red car that I could see. It was quite a scary scene, something out of a horror movie almost. The dream was so scary that I lost my breath and then I told it to go away. I turned over in bed and snuggled up to my husband, hoping the dream would not reoccur. You will soon understand the relevance of this dream.

Peering Over the Sideboard

I had looked forward to meeting up with Caroline and Lyn again. As the climate was now getting much cooler I made sure we had a warm setting in case we wanted to do some healing. The atmosphere was relaxed and calm with gentle music in the background and the aroma of burning incense.

When they arrived we all greeted with hugs. Caroline told us she'd had a vision whilst driving to my house. She said she saw me at the doorstep with a little, blonde haired child standing to the left of me. As we were engaged in this conversation discussing the child's age, I immediately spoke out about Tristen seeing a little blonde haired girl. I also told them about what Dorothea had told me. The same blonde haired child had been seen by a few people now. It was just mystifying. How could so many different people be picking up the vibes of this young girl? Those people had no idea what was going through my mind. What on earth was I to do with her? Did she really feel comfortable around me? Why me?

Lyn always appeared so calm and collected. I truly believe that she is a wise old soul: she seems to have eternal peace. One day maybe I will have that unique quality.

Caroline is very psychic and clairvoyant and has a lovely persona. She is very talented in numerous ways and has much to offer society. I now looked at her as a wise one, she is also very knowledgeable. She wore a lot of Celtic style jewellery and reminded me of someone who would be a new age traveller, going to lengths to stop cruelty to animals, saving wildlife and nature. Almost like an eco warrior.

When we did some healing on one another we noticed the atmosphere in the room change. The energies soared, leaving us with a sense of overall well-being. Giving the feedback was informative. We realised that we were all feeling the same emotions during our progress on our spiritual journey. Simultaneously we agreed that perhaps it was normal to feel a little low at present. Perhaps we were preparing for a leap up to the next level on our journey.

Now we were hungry. Preparing our lunch, Caroline had informed me that she felt someone was upstairs. I agreed with her as I had many spirits as well as angels around the house. She seemed a little uncomfortable for a short period of time. Then we mellowed and chatted about spirits.

It was now an acceptable part of my life that spirits would come and go in my environment. I was able to tell them to leave if I felt too uncomfortable. The angels were by my side to protect me so I did not worry unnecessarily.

Ready to eat our lunch, Lyn sat head of the table with Caroline to the right of her. I was sitting to the right of Caroline. As we were eating our sandwiches I saw a rather astonished look on Caroline's face. She was holding her sandwich close to her mouth with both of her hands when her jaw dropped open. She was staring at the dark wood, mirrored sideboard that was over a hundred years old and had belonged to Daren's granddad. I knew that something had startled her. I was quite anxious to find out what it was. I asked her what she had seen. She gulped her last mouthful of sandwich, reluctant to reveal what it was. I explained I was open to hearing the truth. She then elaborated. A little girl had peered over the sideboard and looked into the mirror. She had blonde hair.

Well, strangely enough, an immediate thought came into my mind about the blonde haired girl in my dream. As soon as I digested the information I had goose bumps all over me. I then revealed my dream from the previous night as we looked at each other mystified.

Was this a message or confirmation of the little girl hanging around the house?

We managed to complete our last session of healing for the day. As time was ticking away we arranged for our next monthly gathering. We found we were benefiting from meeting and looked forward to the next time. Our goodbyes were said with heartfelt universal love.

Recognising a Gifted Child

Little Georgia had been for healing as her mother thought she would benefit. The grief she was coping with since the loss of her father and sister had been masked and hidden and she never had released her grief. I felt I wanted to help her and spiritually felt connected with her. Being brave for her mother she never cried. This child never appeared to be troublesome either. Georgia felt she had benefited from the healing and explained how calm and relaxed she felt. Every time she looked forward to the healing. I felt she was letting go of losing her loved ones. Often she would come for a card reading. Georgia was intrigued to find out if the angels were really looking after her father and sister. The cards would always reveal the correct answer for her.

This eight year old child was gifted and her spiritual talents would blossom in the future to help those who required it. She has undoubtedly already received help from the angels. I feel she is aware of them and is reassured regularly by them.

Georgia had told her mother about her imaginary friends. Her mother was also aware of the support from her daughter's friends and the people she communicated with that are not in the physical world.

Georgia cares passionately for nature and obviously has much love for animals. She had put research and plenty of effort into her school projects and talked about conservation and protecting wild animals. I was very impressed with her knowledge. She spoke very spiritually and is clearly a very special individual who is another old soul.

Healing Connections

Alison, my friend had arranged to come for a healing session. She had no idea of what to expect. The room that was used was always kept to a cleansed standard, ensuring there were no negative energies and making it a sacred space. Prior to the healing we chatted about her sister who was very worried about going for tests at the hospital. At this point of discussing her sister we had no idea what was wrong.

Then I started the healing and became quite aware that Alison could not relax. Continuing the healing I sensed some sciatic pain in her left leg, pain in her spine and in the coccyx. I could also see a stomach and lower intestine. The intestines were revealed a few times so I asked the angels if they were Alison's the answer came back as 'No.' I did not at that moment think too much about why the answer was 'No.'

Overall the healing was good. I had never been made aware of any of the aches and pains this person had. When I gave Alison the feedback, she was surprised.

A couple of days later I telephoned Alison to let her know I had tried hydrotherapy but it made me feel too unwell. We chatted for a while and then she went on to talk about her sister and how she went on at the hospital. I interrupted her to tell her that it was her lower intestine that was causing the problem. Alison was astounded at what I said and enquired as to how I knew. I told her to trust me as the angels always guide me and help me. I had been picking up her sister's health problems when we mentioned her prior to the healing session.

Another healing session for Alison took place at her home. Alison had mentioned she found relaxing a little difficult. Well, I suppose you would if there was a one-year-old toddling around everywhere!

My offer of a simple guided relaxation was accepted. Guiding Alison through the meditation was fine. She went along the winding path and as we approached some trees we rested. I intuitively knew she was hugging a tree. I spoke of her letting go of the tree she was hugging so that we could walk further along the path. After the guided relaxation I did the healing. A message had emerged for her from her grandmother who is on the other side. She wanted to see Alison happy and smiling. This was the lady who never got to say good bye to her grandmother because she was in Greece. Speaking to Alison afterwards she was amazed to find out that I knew she was hugging the tree.

Intuition and guidance from the angels is all I can thank.

Messages are always positive. They are important messages that I believe should be passed on to the person concerned. My messages come via the angels. I am dedicated to their healing energy and wish to complete my duty and service to all souls whom wish to receive help.

21/11

In my solitary hour I meditated in my cleansed room, dedicated to the angels and Jesus Christ. I looked forward to the meditating as I could go into deep relaxation.

Breathing soothingly and letting the gentle music flow as it took me into a space that was so serene. Pale shades of pink and sky blue washed over my closed eye lids. I was in contact with my inner self. Appearing in front of me I saw the numbers 2111. I had no idea the meaning of the numbers at that time. I asked the angels if Sharon was going to pass her driving test. Nothing negative came back, neither did a positive answer. So I relaxed and thought positively anyway.

Past Life Healing

Wei Ling wanted to have her past life healing session done. We sat and chatted, she felt quite excited and I too could feel her excitement.

As we entered her first past life I could clearly see lightning in the sky. It appeared to be in the evening as dusk had fallen. There seemed to be much chaos. Close by, there were people running everywhere. In front, not too far in the distance, was a temple. It was a Chinese temple. The lady I saw running was Wei Ling. I sensed a body with an enlarged stomach; I would estimate that the lady was about five months pregnant. She had the most beautiful face and wore some sort of headdress. The headdress was very delicate with an intricate design in a golden colour. She had made the run into the entrance of the temple. Many others were also making an urgent dash to save themselves. What were they running from was not clear immediately.

Then it was all revealed to me. There was a natural disaster. It was a tornado. Havoc was in the air with gusting winds and the lightning sparking into the distance. Seemingly, quite a frightening experience. Leading into the temple there were some steps and there lay an abandoned bowl. That was all that could be seen. That life then came to an abrupt end and her next life was entered.

Taking me immediately into the next life, I saw a young male in his mid thirties. This was Wei Ling. She had embodied as a male and he was being tortured. The pain was unbearable in his arms as he was tied to some planks of wood. His body was extremely weary, feeling the exhaustion in his shoulders and legs too. The culture did not appear to be Chinese origin, although I still had no idea where he was from. After some time there was a swelling in my throat and I instantly knew this man had been hung since my head drooped to the right of my shoulder. Instantaneously the third life revealed an elderly Chinese gentleman. He appeared very frail but his face could have told a thousand stories. He seemed to be a very wise, innocent man. Watching his delicate face I saw him fall to the ground. He passed away, dying of natural causes. But I knew he had lived a long, happy, fulfilled life. I felt calm and at peace at that moment.

All the past lives had been healed for that session.

I do believe we have many lives to heal in order that we can move on in the present life, to free us of any imbalances in mind, body and spirit.

Let me reassure readers now that there are no complications in the present life, when the past life is healed with the assistance of the angels.

Bringing Wei Ling back into normal surroundings we discussed the session. She was interested to find out more information. Talking about the very first part of the session Wei Ling said she had rapid breathing, which I sensed she had. Not long after this the angels calmed her. However, she did feel sick which I thought was due to the anxiety of the whole experience. I too felt sick after the session. After our discussion about feeling the sensations as the healing was in full flow, we chatted about my own journey on the spiritual path. Wei Ling had left with a different experience of angelic healing.

I understand the healing process carries on after the client has left the healer. The angels helped to heal emotional problems connected with her past life too.

Speaking to Wei Ling the next day she told me that she had felt some minor symptoms, which I explained were the clearing of her previous lives. She was delighted to have had the best night's sleep in a while. That day also she had to deal with a difficult situation and was surprised to see how well she dealt with it, remaining calm, and full of inner peace and uplifted. She was very grateful and quite excited to tell me about this unexpected result.

As much as this friend thanked me, I, in return, thank the angels for their wonderful assistance in making a difference in peoples lives. I am happy and honoured to do this beautiful angelic work.

I had now often wondered why I was chosen to do this. What about my future, when I recover from my debilitating condition. Where does my future go? Where will I be led?

Chapter Nine

No Fear of Talking About Angels

Meeting new faces at the first regional fibromyalgia group was interesting. Initially I was very nervous but shortly after talking to the group leaders I felt relaxed.

People of all ages were present. The room was filled with pain, it was so obviously felt. Other people's pain was entering my body, as if I did not have enough of my own. We were all told we would introduce ourselves and talk about how we were diagnosed with the condition.

Nervousness filled my body as I started to shake. As it was getting closer to my turn to speak I thought about what I was going to say. I had spoken out in crowds of hundreds before now, but mainly children. Now I had lost my confidence. Not communicating on a regular basis told on me. Loss of correct words is a common complaint with fibromyalgia.

Listening to others speak of the years of pain was unbearable. It made me think, was I going to have the pain for the rest of my life? I could not possibly cope with the chronic fatigue, breathlessness as well as fibromyalgia. The reality and fear compressed my heart. I was shocked to say the least and felt down hearted as I gazed blankly. Half-aware now that my turn was nearing I brought my attention back to the room.

Now my turn, I started off with a shaky voice. Once I introduced myself and talked about my family, I explained how I had suffered for a year.

Not worried about sharing my new found talent of healing I told the entire group. Whether they thought I was crazy at that time I did not care.

I have no fear talking about angels and wanted to share the information with everyone. During the break a couple of people spoke to me about healing and told me I had a gift and should use it. At that time I knew I was using it but only for people I knew.

After the next group meeting a lady, Adele, was interested in Angelic Reiki and asked for my telephone number. She told me how much she believed in angels. Between the two of us, a glow of energies was present. I told the lady that I was sure we had met before, her face was very familiar to me. She remarked she had never met me before. I replied we must have met in another life. She became quite giggly and excited.

Within a few days the lady had telephoned me to make arrangements for a healing. She commented how she was looking forward to it.

Message in a Box

The day soon arrived. Adele approached the door. Gingerly she made her way through the front door.

She was in her mid-forties, tall with a slim body frame. To me she appeared quite confident.

We sat in the conservatory chatting and she told me about her father passing away barely 11 months ago. As she spoke about him her eyes filled with tears. I could feel her heartache in my heart centre. As I also had a loss in the family I could empathise with her. She was very sensitive at that time and I realised she needed a listening ear. Feeling her grief as she sat and wept I comforted her with the touch of my hand on her arm. Adele said she had felt tearful and apprehensive a few days before arriving. I explained how sometimes before arriving for the healing itself, the person manifests the symptoms that need to be healed.

She looked at me, bewildered, trying to make sense of what had been said. After a couple of minutes she understood and nodded her head.

After making Adele feel comfortable and having explained the procedure, the atmosphere was calm and ready for the healing.

Once into the healing I could feel Adele's pain in her body. I was able to get rid of the physical pain to the angels as I did not want to be left with it.

The physical pain had lingered with me before now but this time I was able to get rid of it, following the advice from the young healer. While healing was being sent to different areas of the body, I could hear this lady crying. She was just so emotional. I could only send love and calm to her from the angels.

In my vision I could see lots of plant leaves and flowers. The flowers kept reappearing. Then in my view was a crucifix and a box. The mental picture of a box kept flashing before my closed eyes.

The healing had come to an end. Adele had tears as she opened her eyes. Looking at her I knew she was amazed by her experience as she took a deep sigh. She told me there was definitely an angel standing to the left of her. In fact she was adamant that there was an angel present. Although she did not need to convince me because I knew what she was saying was the truth. Adele became overjoyed with the presence and love she felt. I was truly happy for her. She apologised for her many tears in one day. It was not a problem because I understood. During our discussion I was aware that I needed to pass on a message to her from the angels. They were showing the crucifix, flowers and box for a reason and I told her what I saw. She informed me there really was a box that belonged to her father and it did have flowers on it. Inside the box were lots of sympathy cards. She recalled there were cards with crucifixes too. My intuition was to tell her to look inside the box but I made sure that she would only do this at her own pace when she felt ready to do so. I knew there was a message for her in the box.

After a couple of weeks Adele had informed me that she had looked in the box with her elderly mother. She was yet again very excited to speak about her findings. The outside of the box was decorated with beautiful flowers. It held 108 sympathy cards. She went on to say she had randomly put her hand into the box to pick up a card. As she looked at it she said it had a crucifix on it. It was a card from one of her elderly aunts. The card read a thankful message to the family for looking after her brother so well through the years of his ill health. As Adele relayed all this information my heart was overwhelmed with disbelief. She then went on to say more about the second random selection. It was a letter and a poem from her other aunt. The poem described about going to live with Jesus Christ and ended with a few words about now being with the angels. This was quite an amazing experience for me as well as for Adele. We just looked at each other shocked.

Now she said that she looked at things differently and coped better on a day-to-day basis. Well I was very pleased for Adele and her family as she said she felt at peace. Because she felt at peace she said it followed through to her family, too.

Kiss Of Life

Feeling quite unwell with fibromyalgia, I struggled to stand or walk. I had arranged to have a healing session with an ex-work colleague. She was in need of healing for her back pain. She was at a stage in her life where she felt low and a little depressed. Therefore, I could not cancel the arrangement, even though I felt terrible myself.

Sarah, a reserved and quiet person in her mid-twenties, had come to me with an open mind. This lady was not entirely sure if she believed in healing, although she now felt ready to try an alternative therapy.

The room was as usual warm and lit with candles. The incense stick burning frankincense aroma and the angelic music in the background. The fairy lights set a twinkle to the room.

Sarah walked in quite relaxed actually. She always appeared to be calm. Making her comfortable, I was aware I needed to make myself comfortable too.

Seeing is Believing

The introduction went well and then the healing began. After the healing she glowed and left the house looking rather well. I too felt uplifted with a bit more energy than before and overall feeling of lightness.

Soon after Sarah had left I sat with my family at the dining room table eating our evening meal. Glancing over to the room where the healing had taken place Sharon noticed the cherub figurine had moved. We sat mystified as to how it could have moved during the healing session, as I had never touched it. Previously the figurine was facing the conservatory door. It had moved sideways, facing the chair I was sitting on. I understood that it was a kiss of life for me because the cherub figurine is sculptured blowing a kiss. I thanked the angels for giving me the energy to heal Sarah. As Lyn, my healer friend, had said, the cherub was giving me breath. This was life energy. I felt honoured and took it as appreciation from the heavenly realms as my duty for the day's healing had been done.

Making contact with her a few days later I was updated. Sarah was having a lot of dreams, dreams she could now remember. Whereas previous to the healing she had no idea what the dreams were about. I enlightened her, the dreams contained messages and they did have a meaning for her.

This lady has now had déjà vu moments. She thought she had seen a cat in her mother's house, but how could she as her mother was allergic to them? Not long after, whilst visiting her mother, Sarah was amazed to see a cat in exactly the same place she had envisaged. To her surprise her sister had moved back home bringing her cat with her.

Sparkle In My Eye

Having regular treatments with different professionals I was now being told how well I looked. No matter how ill I felt I still had a sparkle in my eye. My spirits were high and I had no reason to complain about my aches and pains. I accepted that with the help from the angels I would be fine. My mood was good, calm and relaxed. 'Just go with the flow' as I would often say to people.

The first time when I was told by Sean, my Bowen Technique therapist that I had a good spirit, I searched to the left of me and then to the right. I thought there was a spirit standing next to me. After Sean watched me do this he said, "No, the one inside you." He was actually referring to my inner spirit. I felt a little silly and naïve, but I took it in my stride. Another person once said 'the windows are the eyes of your soul, you have an attractive spirit.' I was embarrassed to some degree but elated in another as the words were so touching.

The next day I used my oracle cards to find out about my past, present and future. The past card was telling me to honour my true feelings. I knew that was referring to where I would like to be and not to struggle with my feelings in the future. The present card was telling me to move forward fearlessly, which I was now doing and I was beginning to have no fear. The future card was telling me about the magic of nature, to connect with mother earth and breathe the fresh air. Almost like blowing away the cobwebs.

An Appointment with the Doctor

Usually I struggled to get through on the telephone to make an appointment to see the doctor. This particular day I had asked the angels to save me a space with a particular doctor I wanted to see. When I phoned I got through to the receptionist. I asked for an appointment with my preferred doctor and surprisingly I got in to see him as his last patient.

The doctor and I discussed my health and he understood that I was trying different therapies as a means of recovery. He asked how I was really feeling as my mood had been low four months previously. I commented that my spirits were now high. The gentle doctor asked me what I meant and he was waiting for me to elaborate. I sat there wondering how I could tell him I had been seeing angels and feeling their presence. He was a professional surely he would not believe me. He might even think I was mad. After pondering for a few moments I made it very clear I was not crazy and I had not imagined it. I informed him I had seen angels and that I was being guided by them. He took this very well. Well, he did say "Try me, I'm broad minded." I was on a roll: the words just flowed out of my mouth. Giving him time to digest what was said, I immediately thought he was going to bring in the men in white to whisk me away to the psychiatric department of the local hospital. As I waited for his reply I felt a flutter in my chest: I could not distinguish whether it was a good sign or bad. The doctor told me he had heard of people being ill and then feeling uplifted spiritually. Then he commented how some people try complementary therapies such as spiritual healing. He was already aware I had tried this. I was very impressed to see that there was some sort of understanding or even acceptance that the patient should have the choice to venture into other therapies when conventional medicine does not work. I felt that I had spoken out for others who would like to tell their doctors of their visits with spiritual healers. I understand it is not easy to accept for some medical professionals. The doctor was very understanding and I appreciated everything he said. I walked out of the surgery for the first time with a huge smile on my face and feeling wonderful.

The Tick in the Sky

Sharon had now experienced many healing sessions and with her driving test nearing she was not as nervous as before. After another healing session I asked the angels if she would pass her test. Looking out of the window I could see a big tick, it was the marks an aeroplane had left flying through the clear sky. My intuition told me it was a 'Yes', she would pass. I was relatively happy knowing this as we all want our children to reach their potential.

97

Believing is Seeing

A few weeks earlier my aunt had visited. She is also gifted and uses healing for family and friends. Before leaving she gave Sharon a ten pound note. The note had 21/11 written on it. She had no idea that was when Sharon had booked her driving test. But she laughed and said there was a number on it, unsure if it meant anything to us. As Sharon and I looked at the ten pound note with the number on, we were taken aback. However, we did not reveal to my aunt what the significance was.

As it was the day of the test Sharon had some more healing. She remained extremely calm as I did too. Sharon explained how she had not felt this calmness before. As soon as she had left for the test I used the pendulum to find out if she would pass. The answer was 'yes.' I felt happy to trust the pendulum as a warm glow washed over me. Inwardly I was confident. 'Just trust' was being said to me.

A couple of hours later she came home, her face was a red glow. I walked over to the door and as soon as she opened it I knew she had passed her test. We jumped up and down with joy screaming crazily.

Lucy

Fast asleep in my bed lying huddled in my duvet from feet to the top of my head. I felt a pat, another pat and then another pat. The patting was on the duvet, on my head. The patting had woken me. I lay there a little frightened. Subsequently, there was another pat in the same place and then one more pat. I was now wide awake and bizarrely, I knew it was the four year old girl. I mentally told her that I was aware of her presence. The hands were tiny, I could feel that for sure. The pats were given with a little force but still gentle when they touched the duvet. I thought she wanted to wake me for some reason but I did not take a glance. I was too tired and after a short period I fell asleep.

✿ ✿ ✿

After another meeting with my healer he confirmed that the blonde haired little girl was called Lucy. She had passed away following a car accident. He told me she did not want to go to the other side, unsure whether her parents were there to receive her. She did not want to be lonely. Therefore she was quite happy to linger around me. The information was correct and confirmed yet again by a fourth person. Amazing!

I was told she would not be a problem as she was quite happy to remain with us.

Flickering Lights

Sitting reading in my haven, feeling optimistic about my life, I just happened to glance out of the window in front of me when I saw a beautiful glowing light leave the conservatory window. The light had a pure white glow. It appeared at the corner of my left eye, zooming past my left hand side, straight to the glass pane in front of me. It was a beautiful sight to say the least, leaving a calm, peaceful, loving presence behind.

I was awed by this and wondered what it could have been, although I was not sure at this point.

Feeling relaxed, whilst the children were busy playing and working in their bedrooms. I had just finished wiping the kitchen surface when Paula had stopped by. We made a cup of tea and went to sit in the living room when we noticed the ceiling lights were flickering quite eerily.

In the past the lights had flickered as I had noticed the angels were trying to give me confirmation to what I had thought. The simple thought could be 'I need to be more confident.' Then the lights would flicker. But this was different.

My body started to tense and shake, and the lights flickered even more. At that point I became unsettled. My heart began to beat faster and faster. My chest was very tense, and I struggled to take deep breaths. Sitting there I noticed my legs shaking my body felt out of control, I had no idea what to do to settle myself.

I had an inclination that a spirit was trying to use my body to make contact. Who was it and why?

I felt so unsettled that I wanted to ask Paula to leave. Not long after, she did actually ask if she should go as she noticed my manner was not normal. At that time I thought it was rude to ask her to leave as she had not long been with me.

Now I am glad I did not ask her to leave, because something significant was about to emerge. You will shortly find out what this was.

Paula's parents were in their eighties when they passed away. Sadly, both passed away in a gap of eight months, which was a tragedy for Paula. She loved her parents deeply. Like any devoted adult helping their parents cope and live in old age, she was closer to them than ever.

They were a lovely couple, a lady and gentleman with unique qualities from early twentieth century. I always thought Hilda had distinctive etiquette and her overall mannerism was gentle. Roland was a proper old fashioned gentleman, yet again a very warm character.

I knew I had to tell Paula what information was coming through. I told her intuitively that her parents were making contact. She was quite excited and wondered what it was they were trying to tell her. I could sense they were agitated and frustrated. I sensed what they were trying to tell her was that they needed to be released.

Paula had wept often about losing her parents. I would actually say maybe inconsolably. But understanding this was her way of coping. This was grief. This was her love for them. Although, she had no idea of the pain she was causing them by not letting go.

I too have lost someone in my family. This person was my twenty year old sister. I had cried for a long eight years but had no idea what I was doing to her soul. It was her time to go, I realised eventually and knew that I had been stopping her from moving on in the spiritual world. I was pulling her soul to the earthly planes where she no longer belonged. I could feel her presence but was uncomfortable with it. I had counselling, but feel it had not helped as spiritually I did not then understand the process of life and death. I now understand that the person who dies needs to leave the earthly planes so they can be reincarnated or be given a role to play on the spiritual planes. The role could be to act as a guide to loved ones or to reach higher levels spiritually so that incarnation does not need to take place.

Not knowing how to tell Paula, I could not pass this information on. I felt that the situation needed to be given more thought.

The more I asked from my heart if her parents were there, the more the lights flickered. It was like Blackpool illuminations. At that time nothing could stop the lights from flashing. Asking my angels the same question about Paula's parents, the answer always came back 'yes.' Without a doubt Paula and I were convinced of their presence and communication.

Paula had decided to leave not long after as she could see my health deteriorating. As soon as she left the lights stopped flickering, I was astounded.

My body was still struggling to relax. Tension and anxiety remained with me for another hour.

That night I saw a shadow of a man in 1920's dress. He had on a trilby hat and a long crombie coat. This shadow was near the angel on my window, but the man was walking in the opposite direction. I instantly knew that this was Paula's father. He was not going in the correct direction.

I felt that this confirmed what I was thinking. It had not finished here as I still had the task of breaking the news to a grieving woman.

The next day I consulted a colleague to try and help me and reconfirm that I was actually sensing physical symptoms that matched with the spirits' distress on the other side.

It was apparent I was manifesting the elderly couple's distress. Paula's love and grief were ultimately disharmonising their spirits.

I can describe this is as follows: imagine a large sheet of glass. The glass is in the middle of a space. To the right of the glass is the physical world, in the middle is the sheet of glass and to the left is the spiritual world. The person that has passed over is on the spiritual side. The person who is grieving is on the earthly plane, the physical world. Imagine there is a cord, it linked the person on the physical world to the person on the spiritual world.

In this case, the person from the physical world was unable to detach from the person who had passed over. The cord was being pulled to the earthly world every time the person was extremely upset. The spirit then became distressed and frustrated. This spirit did not belong on the earthly planes anymore. It belonged in the spiritual realms. The soul of the person in the spirit world did not need to be attached to the person in the physical world to that degree. The soul wanted to be set free. It wanted to let go. The soul then used a channel to pass on information to be released.

After much contemplation I decided to contact Paula and I was guided by the angels to sort the problem out. Paula had arrived she wondered why I needed to speak to her. As we sat down to talk I could see she was worried. I explained there was no need to worry but it was necessary to pass some information on. As soon as I mentioned how uncomfortable I had felt the other night she admitted it was not my normal behaviour. She encouraged the conversation linking it to her parents. I was empathic as this was a sensitive discussion. Giving this lady confidence to put the matter to rest was the most important thing at that time. I had every confidence that this could be resolved. I gave Paula the option of 'letting go' herself, if she could manage it. Or she could see another healer. If she wanted I could help her to send her parents to the light properly and support her through this emotional time. I accepted as always that the person could see any other healer. There are many healers out there and I feel the client would be drawn to the healer.

Seeing is Believing

Paula had decided she felt comfortable going through the process of 'letting go' with me.

As the day had approached I cleansed the room and meditated for a short time prior to Paula's arrival. As soon as I had finished I noticed a white light leave my conservatory window and go up into the sky. It happened quickly but visibly there.

We had started the 'letting go' of the souls of both parents. It was clearly an emotional time for Paula. She wept considerably but this was just the release of stuck emotions. I knew that she was safe in the presence of the angels. I was guided to do this. Paula trusted me as I trusted myself, with the help of the celestial beings and God.

Sending the souls to the light was beautiful. We finished with a prayer for the two souls to be in the light of God.

The healing took place next with Paula already relaxed. A message was received for this lady to laugh and not cry. Later we sat and talked about the session itself. Now seemingly relaxed with no tears, Paula left.

It was becoming dark so I had put the lamp on to continue reading the book by Sogyal Rinpoche called *The Tibetan Book of Living and Dying*. As I soon started to read the next few lines and read the word 'blessing' I felt a huge hand on my head. The hand was not only big, it was pure love, the presence of it was most definitely there. Instantaneously I knew I had been blessed. It was the hand of God. With this intense feeling of gratitude from the heavenly realms I knew I had done my duty and that it was appreciated. In return I was overwhelmed with the love that was passed down to me. I tried to touch my crown chakra with my right hand so that I could touch the hand, the hand of God, but it was not to be. I hoped even to brush the aura, amazingly the feeling of the hand was disintegrating. I cannot explain how privileged I was.

If you can be touched by anything wonderful, that is the way to be touched! I thanked God for the moment that I will cherish for the rest of my life.

The next day during my meditation I saw the face of Jesus Christ. His face appeared easily in my closed eye view, with his shoulder length hair, his slim face with olive skin. I could only see this great healer for about five seconds before his image faded into the distance and pale shades of violet and creams clouded him. Honoured again knowing that Jesus is with me I felt overwhelmed with a glow in my heart. I am blessed and count my blessings on a daily basis.

Chapter Ten

Meditating

Relaxing to meditate is always an enjoyable experience.

I never knew what I might be shown next during that time. The images came so clearly sometimes.

This particular meditation period was beautiful. Sitting with my legs crossed and my eyes closed in my comfortable surroundings my consciousness drifted. I could see lots of colours purples, pinks and violets in my closed eye view. Splashing and swirling of the colours bringing serenity in my time of solitude. My calm persona sang with peace. The tears that fell from my eyes were those of joy, joy that I had never felt in my life before. The love permeating from the fairies in front of me filled my soul for I am the one who is honoured to see their love, feel their love and live in their love. The auras of angels aglow in my sight help me to transmute fear and resentment from my past. I will always look after myself through meditation, in order to look after those who require guidance, support and healing. I understand the importance of letting go too. We are on a never ending learning curve. Situations arise and therefore issues need to be dealt with. There is always so much to learn. I see that I have much to offer and I want to help people. This is my soul purpose.

Revisit from the Earth Angels

The room was cleansed to welcome the earth angels, my new friends Caroline and Lyn. I looked forward to meeting them both on every occasion.

Lyn had arrived earlier than Caroline. As soon as I welcomed Lyn with a heartfelt hug her own symptoms were emanating into my body. I could feel her back pain, her blurred vision and fuzzy head. I mentioned to Lyn that I felt this as I reached to put the kettle on to boil. Brewing our herbal tea, she told me I was a true healer. I was touched by her words as no one had ever said this before. I regarded her positive comment as a blessing.

Soon after, I removed some of her symptoms from my body with the help of the angels. Now aware that I could alleviate others' symptoms in my own body was great, as I felt I had much more control. However, relieving the other person's symptoms was a bonus. They too appreciated it.

When Caroline arrived we talked about our healing and how we were dealing with the changes in our lives. The three of us need each other and there are significant reasons for us to have met the way we did months previously. Not all is clear, but we are a supportive network for each other so far. We share the same compassion and wish to spread healing. I anticipate there is more to be revealed in the future. Time will tell.

The healing we give to each other was as important as meeting regularly. More often that not, we find that healing was needed in the same areas as before. This is how healing worked, some healing results took longer than others.

During my own healing the two ladies had found some interesting information.

Lyn sat at my left hand side with her hands placed on my heart centre and solar plexus. During the healing itself she removed a weight off my heart centre. I could feel her hand clutching my chest. With her hand I physically felt her remove and clear more of my years of spiritual blockage. However she remarked she did not seem to be clenching anything. But it was definitely felt.

Someone had carried out a voodoo act on me when I was a child it was an aunt. Now many healers revealed a woman was behind it. Still I was suffering with the effects of the awful act on my soul and life. It was revealed that this woman hides behind a mask committing terrible acts. This I know is a fact already. But what has this woman to gain from causing harm to another's soul. It has been extremely difficult through my years of understanding why people like her exist to cause harm to others. I had been told that there was profound jealousy from her towards the family. I will now say that I am stronger than ever before. My spiritual understanding has made me stronger.

I now understand there are polarities. Where there is dark there is also light. Where there is hate there is love. Where there is war there is peace. Light prevails dark. There is much light in the universe now. Light shines everywhere. The many lightworkers all around the world and will shine more light onto our planet and that of others in the universe. The 100% pure light power will banish the darkness one day.

The angels, Jesus Christ and God are with me as I am with them. I will do my best to honour them and serve them.

After our day together we discussed when we would meet again and made further arrangements. I felt quite light in my body, mind and soul after the healing session and was amazed by what Lyn and Caroline had found as it was very true to my life. Our relationship as friends has grown over a very short period of time. Our friendship is yet to blossom. As the cherry tree blossoms, the roots become stronger and deeper.

The Sceptic

Visiting family was a regular occurrence during the Christmas period. It was time to drop off presents to our loved ones across the country. My mother was away visiting my grandmother in Malaysia and was due back this same day.

Gathered at my younger sister's house we allowed the children to roam free and play. The adults sat in the living room.

As usual Paul, my brother-in-law knew how to wind me up. Being a philosophy lecturer he would engage me in a conversation to debate the existence of angels. As usual I would do my best to convince him of my beliefs but he was far too clever and black and white about things. He would put his arguments forward that all is not what the eye can see. Whereas I would argue that seeing is believing. Incidentally, I was the one for many years of my life who never believed until I saw. I could only speak the truth of what I see, hear and the information given. At times I would blank from his conversation and I would call him a non-believer. We chuckled at this quite light-hearted debate. To close the discussion we decided to be amicable and agree to disagree. After the discussion about angels Paul debated whether healing actually works. I could only offer the therapy to him so that he could experience it himself. Guess what, he was willing to give it a try. Now I was flabbergasted. He said he would go ahead as long as I took into account his feedback. Agreeing on these terms the healing session went ahead.

During the session the angels were giving healing to the appropriate areas in Paul's mind body and spirit. Paul was given the option to hear the feedback. He listened with enthusiasm as I relayed the information. His remarks to me were that it was a pleasant, relaxing, enjoyable experience. I suppose that was still a positive feedback. But I felt the healing had gone to a deeper level for him even though he does not realise it. The Angelic Reiki is powerful, bringing healing into the soul. I am sure he benefited from it more than he is conscious of.

Ego Is a Destroyer

Imagine the scene: you are at a celebration where together with other family members you watch the behaviour of two adult sisters, Rachel and Nina.

Just as a spider weaves a web so Nina has created her own view of life based purely on selfishness. Part of her egoism is rooted in wealth. But when she passes over she cannot take it with her. It is just a worldly matter, an illusion of power. In contrast, Rachel has time for other people, with time to listen, to smile, to reassure, time to be a kind and loving person. Which of the two do you think is happier and more fulfilled?

Seeing is Believing

Nina tends to help with the buffet lunch and ushers Rachel out of the room. Nina is jealous of Rachel's new found talents of caring and sends negative vibrations to Rachel's relaxed aura. From the moment Nina arrived she had been rude towards Rachel. Although conscious of the way she was being treated and aware of the problems that would arise if she challenged Nina, Rachel backed down and left the room promptly. Before she left, Rachel and the other family members felt the rage in Nina. It permeated the room with tension.

Knowing that another of Nina's flaws was to sulk childishly when the conversation did not revolve around her, Rachel sent love to Nina even at a distance. An hour or so later Rachel judged the time might be right to make conversation. But Nina immediately became irate. Rachel and the rest of the family were aghast at Nina's reactions. Nina could no longer bear being in the same room as Rachel and excused herself from the party. She disappeared for a long walk.

This is an example of a person whose ego has become so misshapen and enlarged that it becomes destructive. Nina had many issues and she would not tolerate advice. It is the commonly known version of 'I know it all and you know nothing.'

To think selfishly, to act selfishly, and to be in your own existence is always ego based and this is not healthy. The consequences can be extremely destructive. No one feels they can approach the egoist for fear of rejection. The egoist does not know what she has created. There is nothing anyone can tell them, even with kindness and love. Egoists spurn advice and feel they 'have been there, seen it and done it.' Unfortunately though most of us pass on to the other side having not achieved half what we would like to have done.

Real power comes from love. Love is all that we need to cope with life. Love manifests all that is worthwhile; the love of one's partner, children, family members, friends. Remember there are no strangers, only friends we have not yet met. Love transcends all, including ego and fear.

Believing is Seeing

One of the most important things I have discovered is that what you truly desire in life is achievable. Have faith and trust, approach life with love and you will be amazed at what you can achieve.

Full Moon

Since my spiritual journey started I became more and more interested in the full moon. I was just drawn to its magical energy. Awed by the magnificence of something that has been in the dark night sky for billions of years. Lighting our earth, bringing energies that we take for granted, illuminating the darkness on our planet. Now it was my time to appreciate this natural satellite belonging to our planet.

Days before the arrival of the full moon I would become excited and interested in letting go of everything that no longer served me. What a great opportunity for spiritual growth. As I was aware of my major life changes I still needed support from somewhere and even though my family did understand me as a person, they did not quite understand me spiritually. That extra spiritual support came from the sun shining, the fresh air, the wild life in my garden, the sky, the clouds, and the moon energies.

It may almost seem to you readers that I had never noticed before that nature ever existed. I did acknowledge it, but never appreciated it to the level I do now.

Meditating on the day of the full moon to release anything that was out grown and not needed was a special day as I would dedicate the day to 'let go.' I would relax and let my mind settle without too much thought and then mentally converse with my soul to let go of anything that does not serve me. This could have been something simple as the frustration of not recovering, or a fear of moving forward.

I had now come to the conclusion that I would not be working as a teaching assistant again. I was now letting go of any further need of that, so that it would be out of mind completely and making room for my soul purpose. After the meditation of letting go I told God I was ready for my life purpose. I was now ready to do my duty and serve in light.

That particular night as I entered my bedroom I was drawn towards the window. The moon was shining to its fullest. Behind the golden moon shone the rainbow aura. Its beautiful colours were breathtaking. The clouds had formed a shape of wings behind the moon, clearly it was visible. Underneath the moon was an elongated swirl of cloud with a shape of a letter 'S.' At that point I was aware there was a message in the image. Daren was in the room at the time, and I called him over to look at what I could see. When he joined me I told him there was a reason why I was invited to the window. Obviously, he did not share the same enthusiasm as I did.

By now many things had occurred and I suppose he was bored of hearing me discuss angels regularly.

To some degree yes, I can say that the whole phenomena had absorbed me. I had seen too much to brush them off as coincidences, or even to others I might appear to be looking for meanings and signs.

But for me there was a meaning to everything. Everything I was shown was for my own understanding. That is why I feel I want to share this with my readers. There are always signs out there and they are given to us to guide us, for confirmation and even to reassure us. Those of you on a spiritual journey hopefully will understand what I mean. Maybe you yourselves have had visions or signs. Sometimes we are too busy to look at them in a deeper sense.

Not believing what I saw looking out of the window, that message spoke clearly to me. There was a significant meaning. It was a picture from one of Doreen Virtue's oracle cards. It was the card reading, 'Overcoming difficulties.' The card was telling me the worst was behind me as I had faced challenges in my life which made me a stronger person and there would be now new situations arising. That was enough to send shivers down my entire body. I had received my confirmation. I knew that I would have new situations appearing in my direction but exactly when I did not know.

The Miracle Voice

From the first time I saw angels and felt their presence I vowed to have an angel evening to tell others of my newly acquired friends. So cleansing my room for my first angel evening was going steadily. It was only a small affair and manageable. I knew there were a few people interested in angels so I felt I was ready to share my experiences with others. A couple of ex-work colleagues were attending as well as a few more people from other professions. I had decided to tune into the angels so that I could pick out messages for those attending. With my angelic music on in the background I placed my rose quartz and amethysts on the floor. I asked the angels to help me phrase and write the messages in advance. At that time I knew which people were attending but had no personal information at all about those people.

After successfully making my messages I decided to have a rest.

I had now walked over to the conservatory to sit quietly for a while.

As soon as I sat down and closed my eyes, barely for a split second, in my closed eye view I saw extremely clearly Jesus Christ. Jesus stood in full view on a mount with the blue sky in the background. The sky had tinges of light wispy cloud. Standing there in his tall pose, wearing a cream coloured gown with his hair shoulder length dangling near his face. His arms held out at waist height with the palms of his hands facing the blue sky. Jesus was peaceful as he spoke to me. The words he spoke were, "Bring them to me, so they can be healed."

Looking at him as he said these important, valuable words I was numbed. My whole body was a warm glow with calm as I sat motionless.

The miraculous vision had disappeared it may have only lasted ten seconds. Still stunned but calm I knew more than ever that I must heal.

Well, honoured I am. I was given orders by the boss of all healers. I call upon Jesus Christ to assist in my healing and clearly more healing needs to be done still. Thank You, Jesus Christ.

Angel Evening

The energies in the room were high. I put love and only good intention into my messages. These messages were guidance.

As time ticked away, surprisingly I was not nervous. Just before I knew it everyone arrived in their little groups. We gathered in the kitchen dining room. After my introduction about angels in my life we moved onto experiences others had had. Some spoke of people they knew who had encountered guidance from human angels. I was in my element at this point as I have profound belief in the existence and the unconditional love of angels.

The lady sitting next to me was quite nervous and I could feel her shaking. I asked her if she was nervous, she admitted that she was. The nervousness transmitting from this lady remained with me for the rest of that evening. We had now moved on to the topic of deceased loved ones. Between two ladies, an eight year old secret came out. This was something that was very hard to say from one person to the other. It must have been very difficult that it was never mentioned until this day. Tears were shed, hugs and love were given between the two ladies. Everyone sat and listened to a very sad, true story. Sadness filled the room during our conversation of deceased loved ones as many were in tears. With many questions thrown at me I could only answer some through my own experience.

Before leaving we all took a message from the table, which I had previously received and made. We read them out and surprisingly they matched nearly everyone's life. Some were stunned as I saw their eyes fill up with tears. I was aware that not all were corresponding messages but my intuition was that something could still come to fruition for some. The ladies that had attended the evening displayed interest in another angel evening the following month. At that moment I found it interesting, as I had only planned to do the one.

Some ladies that stayed behind were recalling how they felt during the evening. They were describing how they felt brushed with something, although visibly there was nothing there. Some had felt pain, which I explained was a release. Instantly I knew that healing had taken place for the people that attended the evening. They had felt the wings of the angels. One person said she felt cleansed. Well, I was happy to have been able to witness the healing during the Angel Evening. I was now in need of healing myself as my energies were depleted.

I feel as though receiving guidance to continue the awareness of angels was growing. I should do this. It is not negative if I feel drained because I will recover. This is my way forward. This is part of my spiritual journey.

Say A little Prayer

December 7th was always a sad day for me as it would have been my sister's birthday. She was a year older than me, wise and beautiful. Passing to the spirit world, leaving an eighteen month old baby girl behind, was very difficult for all the family to cope with. No mother, father, sister or daughter should have to go through such a tragic loss or circumstances. Crying for years did not help anyone.

Knowing what I know now about life and death, it is simple. We plan to come into our chosen family, to learn lessons and for those around us to learn from us. This means that we choose our family even if it has chosen to be a dysfunctional family. This however as I believe is not the wrong choice but for those involved to learn from each other. It is merely our life lesson. Our plan is made before we arrive on the earthly planes. When a person passes to the spiritual world, they do not die in soul, only in body. As Diana Cooper mentions in her books 'the caterpillar has merely grown wings to fly, it has transformed.' We will see them again, be it in another incarnation or in the spiritual world itself.

As children my sister and I argued as sisters do, we never always saw eye to eye. We used to fight, about who wanted to be which character when playing families. As adults we worked together and became very close, we had a proper friendship as well as relating as sisters. Her traumatic death led me to guilt and wondered why it was not me who had died. Why did God take away this lovely person, how would we all cope? How would her child grow up having neither parent to love, support, and care for her? It was not fair.

A few days after her death she approached me, dressed in white, in my house. Too scared at that time I could not cope with the apparition.

Now I understand that there was absolutely nothing we could have done to save her, it was her plan.

She is looking down on us and maybe not too far away.

I regularly say a little prayer. Through meditation, I know she is around me. Lighting a candle and sending a prayer her way on her birthday is fine as I accept her death now. I know she is in peace now because my intuition tells me so.

When I had previously met my healer friend Lyn, she told me her father was very ill. He was not given long to live by the doctors. He was an elderly gentleman in his eighties.

This particular morning, around 10.30, I had an urge to telephone Lyn. Speaking we discussed how her father was dying and had survived without fluid intake for over a week. She continued to say how bizarre it was at his age, as his pulse was still strong.

Immediately my breathing became difficult. The same anxieties were following through as with Paula's parents. I explained to Lyn the anxieties that I was experiencing were actually her fathers, not my own. Lyn apologised if I felt uncomfortable. I told her not to worry as my health would be fine.

I started to receive important information for Lyn. The words were flowing out of my mouth.

Lyn had got a pen and paper to write the information down as it was spoken very quickly. She was told that there was unfinished business. Things were not clear. There was need to forgive from all parties. The family needed to meet the father individually. This person was not going to pass over until this was done.

His soul was not prepared to leave. The death needed to be as peaceful as possible. No distress, it was important to create a tranquil environment, to play healing music, to have healing crystals at his bedside. Creating such a serene atmosphere was just as important as saying goodbye.

After giving this message I could feel calmness as my breathing slowed down and the anxieties disappeared. I told Lyn the information was given so that her father could pass away peacefully. She understood this needed to be done. She informed me she was going to the hospital shortly. I told her I would send a little prayer for her father to take him to the light, as well as sending a prayer for the family. She appreciated everything that was said. I knew he would pass away that day.

The uncomfortable feelings I had whilst giving Lyn the message disappeared shortly afterwards. Yet again, I knew I had done my duty as I felt a three foot warm glow around my body. I had been vaccinated a couple of days earlier against flu and pneumonia. It was confirmed by the nurse that I had an allergic reaction to the vaccination. I did at that point know that I did not need it after all. Since having the vaccination I had felt a little ill but the glow around my body was unbelievable.

At six o'clock the same evening, I asked the angels if it was a good time to send a prayer for Lyn's father. I had actually received the answer; it was a blue cross in my closed vision, meaning 'no.' Shortly afterwards I was watching television when a song came on, it was 'Somewhere over the Rainbow' from the film, 'The Wizard of Oz.' Listening to this song I became very emotional. Sitting sobbing in my living room, the song made a deep impression on me. I realise now that it is a very spiritual song. This explains why it is a favourite film of mine even to this day.

I asked again if I could send Lyn's father to the light, the answer was a tick, meaning 'yes.'

I cleansed the room with my Aura-Soma sprays and lit a candle. With my gentle angelic music on in the background I was ready to send Lyn's father to the light. I had encased him in pure white light sending him to the heavens above with peace and love. The prayer was said simultaneously, visualising his soul departing the earthly planes to the spiritual.

Within the next hour I received a message from Lyn to say that they had all spent time with their father, the energies in the room changed and he passed away peacefully within that hour and with all the family present. I had a peaceful moment myself at that time reflecting on what had happened it seemed like something miraculous had taken place.

Lyn phoned to say she truly felt I was a messenger from God to have given that information, she appreciated the help. I was only too happy to assist.

In the night I was awoken by the angels showing me a golden path, it was flowing just like water. Then in my view I saw angel wings and shapes of hearts. This was a message to tell me I was on the flow of a golden path with the love of the angels. As ever I would wake and note everything that was shown to me. Glowing with their love I knew I was on the right path. I was living my life purpose.

This now strangely takes me to my past. Growing up I had always felt close to the elderly. The elderly were my friends. They may well have been in their seventies and eighties but I resonated with them. I took time to check up on the mature ones, to fetch them their groceries or sit and chat with them, to make them a cup of tea. Or even spare time to listen to them groan about everyday life.

One day an eighty-six year old friend of mine became ill and was admitted to hospital. As I was then working as a volunteer in a school I did not manage to see her quite as regularly. The lady had apparently called for me and I was getting ready to leave for the hospital I was told she had passed away. This lady only lived a few doors away. I was devastated and I pondered for months wondering what she wanted to tell me. I had become quite frustrated as my other neighbours knew of the message but did not pass it on.

As soon as I knew that people were ill and dying I had an overwhelming urge to be by their bedside even though I did not like death or understood it.

It was the same with Lyn's father I just wanted to be there, not quite understanding why. But it all makes sense now as a respected gentleman I know told me I could be a soul transformer. Well this made much sense as I felt I could send souls to the light. Having done this successfully with a few people already, as guided to do so by the angels, the process benefited those grieving as well as those who had passed away. The people involved have looked at their lives differently since transferring the soul of their loved one to light. They have felt much calmer and have been able to carry on with their lives.

Too Ill To Cope

Bob, my friendly neighbour had telephoned to say he wanted to speak to me. It was Bob's wife Anna who had passed away about nine months earlier. I was feeling too ill but could not turn him away as he needed support and someone to talk to. Still hanging on to the telephone, as he spoke I was becoming more and more drained. Just speaking to him made me breathless although I had not been breathless prior to the call. The telephone had cut off 3 times and I instinctively knew the angels were helping me so that I would not be drained of energy. I was weak and could not cope with another deceased spirit being channelled through me. I just did not have the strength. Before the telephone could be cut off again he said he would like to come and see me. I agreed as I would now have an hour to rest. From that point onwards I felt worse but did not have a contact number to cancel his visit with me. Sitting in the conservatory with my angelic music on in the background I did some meditation. I had done all that I could to make myself feel a little better before Bob would arrive. Not feeling much improved, I sat and waited for the door bell to ring. The time arrived and still there was no Bob and after a couple of hours passed I knew he was not going to appear.

I used my oracle cards to see what message I would have from the angelic hierarchy. It was clear, as the message on the card was telling me to retreat until I felt stronger. Well this explained why Bob did not come to see me as he said he would. Usually he kept to his word. I sat thinking there was a reason for this. Then it dawned upon me that the angels were keeping him at bay as I felt weak. I had felt drained before in his presence. It was not just that, Anna's spirit was using me to give a message to him which in due course left me weakened.

I planned to do nothing more for the next few days other than to rest.

Chapter Eleven

Gorilla in the Mist

After days of feeling absolutely exhausted, I woke up one morning still not feeling my confident self.

Taking a shower was cleansing for my spirit as I believed it would take any negativity away from the previous day. Sometimes I felt others' negativity lingered with me as well as my own infrequent negativity.

The morning was quite dark, as it was still winter. Waking to find my husband had left the house to go to work, I decided to use the shower before the children woke up, or as usual there would be a queue. After showering, I noticed there was a lot of steam and mist in the bathroom. Glancing over at the misty glass window I could clearly see an image. The image was that of a gorilla. The gorilla was clearly showing a sad face. The face was beautiful even though it had sad eyes peering at me and with no smile. I could even see the colour silver on his chin and forehead. This was definitely a silverback gorilla. Now, wondering why it had been shown to me I went back a few times during the break of dawn to see if there was a further message to be revealed. Showing it to my eldest daughter, Sharon, she admitted there was an image there. The sun had risen and then I could no longer see the primate. Subsequently, I was led to the computer by instinct to check on the website for silverback gorillas. I wanted to find out what their spiritual meaning might be. Sharon helped me to do this. To our surprise it was there. The spiritual meaning for a silverback gorilla was 'communicating with the dead.' Well 'blow me down,' I thought, what a revelation. This linked in with the days previously with Bob's deceased wife Anna and with helping Paula. This gorilla had confirmed that I had been communicating with the dead.

Sitting in my living room having a bite of my sandwich I could see clearly the face of gorillas. Their faces were visible in the velour trodden on rug. Also that evening a documentary came on the television about saving gorillas from extinction. I understood that these were all relevant reminders of my communication with past souls. For many mornings to come I was to see the same primate faces.

Was this animal trying to tell me something else? If so I did not know what.

Days later, I noticed some hand prints on my mirrored wardrobe. I wondered why they were in such strange positions. One was upside down at a height that would have been difficult to print by a family member. Strangely these peculiar prints made me wonder if they were a reminder of the gorilla. I know it may sound very silly to say a gorilla had made the prints, but there was no way any of the family could have made those awkwardly positioned prints. Perhaps it was reminder of the gorilla's presence.

Surprised

Later that day I decided to meditate. Sitting in my usual surroundings, the room purified and gentle music to take me away from my surroundings, I began to let go of my physical awareness.

I allowed myself to be absorbed into the serenity and tranquillity of the music. Whilst in this peaceful state I saw the face of Jesus Christ, then the face of other Ascended Masters. This was all very comforting for me. I felt honoured, loved and guided. This is what Dorothea was trying to tell me, they were all there for me! The Ascended Masters Saint Germain and Djwal Khul also had a very special connection with me months before I realised who they were. I felt as though I had a part to play on their behalf. This was to heal others, to direct others and to help others through their transformation. At this time they were appearing to me to help in my own direction and transformation. I had now looked forward to their appearance and had great respect for these Masters for appearing to me on such a regular basis. After the meditation I felt very shaky but I thought it was due to my vaccinations I had weeks previously.

Feeling exhausted I went to bed in the afternoon, as I had to do regularly to have my rest. Lying there I meditated in complete silence. I fell asleep but awoke to a vision. In my closed eye view I saw some gold coins. Lyn's name appeared with a 1 and 2 nearby. Opening my eyes I could still see the same mental picture. I glanced at the clock it was 4.18pm. I liked to check the time, to see what I was shown, in case there was any significance. At this time I could see no significance at all but intuitively I was told something special was going to happen for Lyn in the next year or two. I was quite excited to have seen this for her and could not wait to let her know. The whole vision was visible for at least a couple of minutes after opening my eyes. It was lit in pure gold. The experience of the vision itself was enriching

On waking I was contemplating whether or not to go ahead with the next healing session. I knew I had little energy but could not let Gina down. Gina was an ex-work colleague. Consulting my oracle cards I was informed I had to forgive a family member with whom I could not speak to due to a lack of understanding with both parties. I did this mentally by sitting quietly. As soon as I had forgiven, my energies returned slowly. I was quite amazed at this task. I then decided to let go of any guilt connected with the healing session with Gina as I felt I had to cancel. I was supposed to heal whether I felt well to do so or not, this was to be my path. I knew I would recover as I would receive healing too.

Before Gina arrived the room was made ready for her. It was never a chore to purify the room as it was now part of my everyday life. I accepted this happily.

Gina had bought me a little angel gift which was ideal as I loved anything concerning angels. Gina was unaware of how I worked so we discussed the healing and my own particular method. She was quite relaxed as the healing took place. After the session she became very emotional as the angels informed me of someone close to her passing away. She had revealed just 3 weeks prior her close friend had passed away and she was obviously still grieving. Her life was unfolding before her, she was somewhat surprised. Amazed by what information was given she accepted the help and was grateful for the session.

I have truly felt that my life path is to help others and that is satisfying and fulfilling for my soul.

Symbols

I had fallen into a deep sleep but suddenly I woke and was engulfed by a golden colour in my closed eye view. The gold background soon showed me a pure deeper coloured gold star. It shone very brightly for a few seconds. After that I was given the image of a spiral. The spiral was yet again outstanding on the slightly paler coloured background. Shortly after the spiral was shown, a big bright sun appeared. Seconds later an angel was shown to me and then a phoenix in flight. It was fantastic, I could not believe it. I checked the digital clock it read 4.18am. My heart was full of joy. Every part of these symbols had a message which all made sense to me.

This was quite something. It had no comparison to dreaming. I knew the message would be powerful. The star is in the meaning of my name Parveen, a cluster of stars. The star also means knowledge of good and truth. The spiral is a symbol of healing and the sun a symbol of sun energy, the angels were my help and the phoenix meant 'break free, transform and fly.'

The message came through as, 'Parveen heal with the angelic energy, transform and break free.' I felt fantastic and confident that this could be achieved. Telling my family I was very excited. I needed them to trust me and believe me. I can do it.

Ready to meditate in the afternoon, sitting in my living room whilst in solitude, I placed a blanket around my legs to keep me warm as I was feeling very shivery. It was winter, although the room temperature was warm enough, I still felt cold. Sitting ready to start my meditation I took a few gentle breaths. Without a doubt I had become deeply relaxed. After some ten minutes or so I heard large, heavy footsteps in my bedroom. Listening carefully I heard small patters too. Even though I knew there were friendly spirits in the house I still became a little on edge. Knowing fully that I was not imagining the footsteps I decided to calm myself down. There was no need for the fear. I suppose I was alarmed and was just not expecting the noises to start when I was so deeply relaxed. I knew I would be fine as the angels were around with their pure energies. I had slowly let go of my surroundings again. Within another few minutes I went into a vision. I could clearly see a lion and lioness. They were both running in the same direction. They were a beautiful golden colour. The scene itself was great to observe. The message was clear, that by being brave and having courage anything could be achieved. It was not a day dream, but a vision. I wondered if I was to see the visions regularly when meditating. But I suppose I would have to wait and see.

During another meditation in the tranquil setting of my living room, I could see a symbol. After investigating the symbol a little, I found out it resembled the Ancient Symbol Caduceus. I found out that this symbol meant 'Messenger of God' and 'Conductor for the dead.' Grounding is when one is anchored to the physical planes whilst in any meditative state. I intuitively received this, 'with my physical self grounded, I was now connecting with my heart chakra.' The colour green washed in my view. The healing heart was ready and my physical body grounded in order for more healing to take place.

My symbol resembling ancient symbol Caduceus

Now having more than one vision or message in the night was becoming common.

After having my personal message revealed to me I saw a shoe. It was a ladies' formal shoe. I am sure you ladies out there will understand what I am getting across to you. There are the evening shoes that would be worn to go out for meals and parties. There are sandals for evening wear. There are casual day shoes. But then, there are formal shoes that are worn at meetings and interviews. Well I only possess one pair of formal shoes that I wear for interviews and meetings. These shoes I will call my business shoes as that is when they are worn most often.

The image revealed to me was of my business shoe. I was only shown one. I checked to see what time it was. The clock read 3.04am. That vision was still in full eye view when my eyes were open. As I closed my eyes after a few minutes I could still envisage my shoe. Sometime later it dispersed into the purple background of my closed eyesight. The meaning of my shoe revealed 'go into business.'

Not long after I fell asleep again, thinking that was all I needed to be informed of, but I was woken up again at 4.18am. After checking the time I wondered what they wanted me to know this time. I was amazed by the beauty of the colour gold once more, the phoenix appeared flightless in my view, then I could see the sun shining and then cherubs were floating. Shortly after staring at the cherubs the phoenix reappeared in flight and beautiful, pure golden angels were surrounding the phoenix.

Awed and amazed by the beauty of the vision I felt warmth and excitement washing over me. I truly was receiving guidance and reassurance about my life. The guidance had to be from The Divine. As I explain how it was all seen it might be difficult for readers to visualise. Have faith that it was pure love and reassurance from the heavens.

The message was that with the sun's energy, I will be transformed with the help of the angels. The flightless bird will fly with assistance from the angels and this in turn linked some sort of business they had planned for me. At this moment I had no idea what business they wanted me to follow.

If you could be guided, well how about receiving the guidance from the Creators Messengers?

My messages are often heard through music, whilst I am driving. The lyrics in a song are there to remind me that I am doing fine. After healing a person I would here the song 'The Only Way Is Up' by Yazz, another song 'No Worries No Worries' by Simon Webb, and then 'Angels' by Robbie Williams. I could not ignore that these were just songs being played on the radio. Each song was giving me a message. They were all symbolic. Usually the songs came in a row of three with the important messages. I thanked the angels for their messages of support and reassurance.

Love Conquered Fear

On my way to see the healer I found that I was being prevented from reaching him. There was nothing physically stopping me. It was a spiritual form of fear. This fear manifested into physical symptoms. The symptoms were not feeling well enough to be travelling, feelings of collapsing, anxiety and the unknown reason for the visit to the healer. What was going to happen during the session? Or did I already know something positive could emerge? Is that why fear was trying to stop me?

Driving along I was now urged to go back home. My breathing became difficult and I was getting pains in my chest. I had made my backup plan for Daren to rescue me from the lay-by near the dual carriage-way.

I knew I had to overcome something but what was it? My energies were being drained. I just wanted to cancel this appointment. But somehow I knew I also had to be there for my progression. Was it all going to be worth it? I was sure nobody would put themselves through this much distress to see a healer. The ideas of heading back home seemed so much easier. I had every excuse as I felt so unwell.

A part of me kept saying 'go ahead you need to be there.' But the majority was telling me I was not fit to do anything. This was just torment. Why was this happening to me? Why?

As I came nearer and nearer to the healer's house I felt more and more unsettled. My breathing was disturbed. I felt I was going to pass out. I had never felt this ill before whilst driving. I thought I would need to pull over to rest. The symptoms, yes, do sound very similar to that of anxiety but I was not convinced that was it. This was a deep down spiritual issue. It was a battle.

Glancing at the digital clock on the dashboard I saw the time was 13.13 and the temperature on the dashboard also read 13 degrees Celsius. An immediate calmness rushed over my body leaving a warm glow. I was baffled at this stage as all of the ill feelings had now left my physical body. Parking up outside the healer's house I became so emotional. I had tears in my eyes. These were tears of confusion and joy; I was overwhelmed by the most bizarre experience.

I knew what the number 13 symbolised; it was the number of Ascended Masters, those masters whom I regularly see around my house. The number 13 was visible 3 times. They were supporting me through the ordeal. They were reassuring me I would be fine. Giving my gratitude to the Masters was the least I could do.

As the healer welcomed me into his house I was still trying to gather myself. I told him of the difficulties I encountered reaching him for the healing. Instantly he told me that it was fear trying to stop me as I was about to make major life changes. This all made sense to me as I had seen the number 55 an awful lot. The number signified major positive life changes. The visions of the phoenix also linked with my transformations, just days previously. It was ironic how this was all building up.

The healer explained this was an important time as I was there for a reason, to let go of anything that did not serve me. I suppose I was a little nervous. What was I going to let go of?

As I entered the healing itself I saw the lion running again. It was running with courage. I knew I had healing for any underlying anxiety and nervousness towards reaching this point. The colour gold appeared in my vision it was a very pure gold. I knew at that time that something special was taking place.

I also felt something being removed from my lungs as well as my heart. Almost like having an operation. I thought to myself, 'Just give me something to numb the pain, I need an anaesthetic.' I must admit it was rather painful but I needed to go through this. I wanted to shout 'Stop' at one stage. My intuition told me to persevere. My gut instinct would not allow me to shout out. After a while the feeling and pain subsided. When I came back to the surroundings of the therapy room I could clearly see a golden aura around the healer. I was told that I looked different. I was told I had seemed different. I thought I was just the same old me, but he could see something different in me. To some level after thinking things through I realised that I had received some special healing. I had come away feeling and lighter in mind, body and spirit.

✿✿✿

A couple of ladies had been for healing and I spoke to them about their emotional well-being as they needed some healing so I decided to send them distant healing.

Speaking to Gina, she was a little distressed and concerned with the situation her son was in. He had become a little too much for his parents to cope with. Obviously teenagers are nowadays becoming more opinionated and want life to be their way. I did not need to know too much as it was their business. So with her permission I offered my assistance. I sent the teenager some healing to help him calm his ways. Only the next day the teenager had walked down the stairs to tell his parents that he had a dream. It was vivid and he was spoken to by an angel telling him to be good as they are watching him. His mother blindly listened to him and watched him take a different approach. He had surprised her by making her cups of tea and telling her to take her rests regularly. That was a sudden, short and effective transformation for the family, noticeably appreciated. Thank You Angels, you can make miracles happen.

The next day I felt optimistic about my future, it was just a knowing or should I say claircognizance.

Time for bed and I had not managed to do my meditation. So I thought I would do this just before falling asleep. Closing my eyes I saw a vision of Gandhi. It was very clear. Mahatma Gandhi's head was bald, his eyes twinkled and his spectacles sat on the bridge of his nose. His frail, bony frame showed his collar bone with just a glimpse of his white shawl wrapped around part of his shoulder. I wondered why I was shown this vision or why he was presenting himself to me. I knew he was a great peace leader and a speaker for freedom. Perhaps he made me aware of him as I had helped to make peace within Gina's household.

Perhaps he was there to tell me I was now in peace and free.

Nevertheless, I was honoured to see the great leader and proud to have met him.

We can have everything but have nothing. We can have love and have nothing. Love conquers fear. Love conquers negativity.

The Universe

Falling asleep, reaching the relaxed state and then deep in sleep I was woken up by something I had never seen before. The vision was pure gold in colour just like the other visions I had had recently. But this would beat the rest.

Amazingly, I could see the universe. Describing it could never be put into context.

The backdrop was pure gold with lots of stars in the distance. Some stars were bigger than others, some shone brighter than others. The vastness was incredible. What a view! Is this what astronomers can see when in space, I thought? The view was very real. The word 'cosmic' came to my mind instantly.

As I opened my eyes I could still see the universe. Looking at the digital clock it was 12.30 am. Astounded by the magnificence I did not want to stop seeing this phenomenal view. Closing my eyes I wished to continue the panorama.

Shortly onwards, I was in the middle of a ceremony. It was all taking place in a white view. Everything was white, the people, the trees, the buildings. I wondered where I was. It was no where I recognised on the earthly planes. People were standing in crowds.

Seeing is Believing

They were all dressed in white gowns so it appeared. There was calmness, the vibes were pleasant. Every one of us was watching a speaker on a balcony. The speaker was a male wearing a headdress and a cloak type gown. Upon the balcony were also other people, a couple of ladies and a couple of men. From the crowd I could see this important leader. He was giving valuable information but what I did not know. This was an important time for all to be gathering. There was a lovely feel from the crowd. I can honestly say that I do not even know what language was spoken. Shortly afterwards the pure white scene was dispersed into the purple coloured background.

Obviously I was taken aback by this remarkable scene. I lay there awake for sometime knowing I had received some sort of knowledge. Even though, the reason for the vision was not crystal clear. I felt I had received wisdom. I had no idea at that time why it was enfolding before my eyes. Then out of nowhere the Star of David appeared in front of me, while wide awake I watched it in the golden shade. Eventually I closed my eyes as I became tired. I knew that the healer had told me he saw something extraordinary but could not describe it, I wondered if it was this.

Sleeping until the early hours of the morning I thought of why that scene had been revealed to me.

Not long after my thought, I was woken to see a scene out of the epic film 'The Wizard of Oz.' It was in full colour format. The scene that was being played was the part when the scarecrow was scratching his head and the wizard had passed him a scroll of papers. On the scroll papers was the information as he had no brain.

Whilst watching this I was told I had been given some important information. The important information was that I was once in the city of Atlantis. I was once, many life times ago, one of many whom lived in peace and harmony.

How special did that feel, I was lost for words. What was Atlantis? I needed to find out more about this peaceful place.

The following day, feeling exhausted and fatigued, the family and I were supposed to watch 'The Nativity Story' at the cinema. After much contemplation and rest I was helped by the family to make this trip out.

Arriving at the cinema we entered to find only ourselves and another family occupying the whole of the cinema. Surprised I was, wondering where everyone was. Nevertheless, I looked forward to watching the film.

As the story unfolded I became very emotional. Tears streamed down my face. I tried to stop myself from crying but my emotions poured out even more so. When the angel appeared to Mary in the film, she told herself that no one would ever believe her. I took a big gulp as a lump formed in my throat. That was exactly how I felt, how would anyone ever believe me? I see these visions and receive guidance from the angels regularly, but would anyone ever believe me?

After thoroughly enjoying this wonderful film, we returned home. Daren and the children prepared the evening meal. I needed a rest, so I meditated in my bedroom.

As I meditated, just for a short time, I saw beautiful golden angel wings. The wings were my confirmation of my thoughts and reassurance that they believed me and what I see is truly there. Feeling of support and faith from the angels made me smile. I talk freely of the angels. Some people understand me and some do not but I know the angels are here. My will is to make others aware of these celestial beings.

Understanding the Message

It was time to meet the other earth angels. We greeted each other with a hug. Ready for our morning coffee we sat talking about how we had been getting along since the last time we met. Feeling a bit under the weather did not put me off talking. As usual I had plenty to say!

Seeing is Believing

Lyn bought the coffees and placed them on the square table. As she sat opposite me I started talking. She was interested in what I had to tell them and became engrossed in my tale. Caroline burst into fits of laughter. Unaware of why she was laughing I had to ask her. She told me that I never came up for air, one sentence rolled into the next. Well that was true. But I felt I had been ill for over a year and could not speak much as it was too painful to talk. So I thought I was making up for lost time. I am sure that my husband would disagree. After our giggle and seeing the funny side of things we moved on for lunch.

The garden centre was quite busy as it was Christmas time. A lady sat playing the piano, which brought a lovely feel of seasonal good will. As many shoppers gathered for Christmas lunches there were not many tables vacant. We were lucky to have found a small table to seat the three of us. Feeling rather hungry we decided to have a healthy soup. Listening to someone play the piano was a rare occasion whilst having lunch. Many traditional Christmas carols were played.

Whilst we were engaged in conversation the angels were asking me to pay attention to the song. I rudely interrupted the conversation the two ladies were engaged in and I asked them to listen to the tune that was being played as it had a message for us. Looking at each other we tried to hum the tune, trying to figure out the lyrics, it was quite comical actually. After a couple of minutes or so it was all coming together. The odd words were sung and a few were missed out as we sat nodding our heads trying to sing the words. Then there it was the chorus. The song was sung by Michael Jackson called 'Heal the World.' The angels were telling us that was what we had to do, to make our world a better place.

We sat looking at each other, and each one of us felt cold shivers run through our body. It was uncanny. The message itself spoke volumes to us.

The time we were to share had come to an end for this particular day. We parted and said goodbye and made our way home.

Believing is Seeing

✿ ✿ ✿

Bob had come round for a chat. Whilst we sat talking I was getting the feeling that Anna wanted to make contact. I was no medium but it was that unsettled feeling I was getting again. He had not said his goodbyes properly and she was not settled. Bob had found life difficult. He was trying to move on but things were not going to plan. He admitted that before Anna's departure everything flowed for him. He could not understand why things were not moving on in his life as he wanted them to. I invited Bob to go through the 'letting go' process with me properly. He understood the information that I had given him, and we carried out this simple but effective procedure with the help of the angels. Bob was ready to see his life settle again. He left feeling quite calm.

Being empathic about situations I believed if someone was suffering help should be offered. If it is suitable for those involved then it is right to give help. This is generally how I have always worked.

✿ ✿ ✿

One particular evening the family were all sitting in the living room. It was 8.30pm and as I had become quite tired and was prepared to get an early night. Sitting next to Daren I had mentioned doing this. He commented that we should all watch a family film as the children were on their Christmas holidays. Persuaded to do so I sat fixed in my comfortable position. The film had started and the rest of the family sat with enthusiasm to watch the television. Part way through Daren started to read his mountain climbing book. The film on the television became distorted. I sensed this was a message via the electricity. As Daren got up to leave the room, the film on the television continued to flicker. My children were frustrated as they were missing the film. I told Daren the angels were letting him know that he was the one who wanted us all to watch the film but he sat reading and now he was the one getting up to leave. They were reminding him it was his idea now he was not fully participating.

Daren turned round and spoke to the television. He said "Ok, I'm just going to make a cup of tea."

Instantly the television was back to normal working order. Looking at each other we agreed it was the angels communicating. I silently thanked the angels for their reminder to Daren.

Retiring to bed after the film I managed to do some self healing. I could clearly see the stars twinkling in the universe. It was beautiful to see the image again. After the healing I fell into a deep sleep. All night I dreamt of dogs. The dream signified fulfilling my soul purpose even though I had self doubt and uncertainty. I could do this but as humans we all have some self doubt about whether what we want to do is achievable.

At that time I knew I wanted to heal but to what level I was unsure of. What was going to come my way, I was unsure of too.

✿✿✿

Meditating was always a way of connecting to my inner self. Sometimes I would be fortunate to receive guidance and messages and sometimes I would not. My messages from electricity were always interesting. With a book of angel number guidance I could interpret the meaning.

My daughter had electric hair straighteners which had digital numbers that would appear as a reference as to how hot the equipment would get.

Straightening my hair I glanced at the number on the appliance, it was as though I was called to look. The number read 177; it had a meaning which I needed to look up in Doreen Virtues *Book of Angel Numbers*. The message was telling me that my positive thinking had guided me to my right path. Also telling me the angels were pleased with my courage and it would be inspirational to other people. Looking this up in the angel numbers book I knew it was true to how I had recently been feeling.

Believing is Seeing

✿✿✿

My friend Alison L came to visit me. As she sat on my sofa talking to me her anxieties were emanating into my body. I told her I was sensing the anxieties. She understood why the anxieties were there.

Alison had spent an hour with me, dusk was falling and she was now ready to go home. As soon as she left the front door I went into the kitchen. In the darkness I could see my angel and lotus flower glowing. They stood on a battery operated stand which shone beautiful coloured lights. The crystal ornaments poured out the chakra colours, the red, the orange, pink, green and blue. The conservatory door had been locked and the children were upstairs. No one had been into the conservatory. How could they have been turned on?

The angel and the lotus are both used in my method of healing. Instantaneously I knew that someone Alison and I had spoken about needed healing. The angels were bringing the person to me.

Looking into the conservatory I stood staring and thinking for a couple of minutes. I made the decision to contact Alison. She told me it could be her boyfriend. They had arranged to visit me.

Shaun may have been sceptical about my experiences but he was open-minded to have a trial session of healing. I was impressed with his decision. The healing went very well for him. He told me he felt relaxed. After the pair of them left I received a text message from Alison saying he was very happy. She wondered how long it would last as he was very different, she had noticed the happiness in him. I was pleased to see some effect but could not guarantee any time scale for the positive result.

✿✿✿

I had been stuck indoors for quite some days now and longed to be outdoors for a short while. The dizziness made me feel as though I was on a roundabout.

Seeing is Believing

A couple of nights previously whilst in bed asleep, I had strange feelings of floating in an upright position. This linked with my dizzy feelings. I grounded myself to mother earth as best as I could. I was aware I was undergoing some major spiritual transformations. I recognised this sort of vertigo as it had occurred many years ago after giving birth to Alysha, my youngest daughter.

It was just like being on a ship riding the rough stormy sea. Grasping on to whatever was in sight to keep some sort of balance and waiting to be rescued by the change of calm weather.

Daren cooked breakfast as I tried to rest. As good as he was to do the chores around the house I could do nothing but wait for the storm to end. I even struggled to eat the breakfast that was cooked for me. My children were excited to go into the town centre to buy a few items. Daren had promised the children a hot chocolate. I wanted to be part of the family trip out. Quite upset I realised that nothing could be changed, not that day any way. Feeling sorry for myself I decided to have a time of meditation lying down. The meditation did not last too long as I felt too dizzy for even what I enjoyed on a daily basis. I tried to read but the words were spinning away from my eye sight. After giving up reading I became very tearful and a little angry with God. I stood up shouting, "God, why do I have to keep going through illnesses, my whole life I have been through challenges and difficulties. Have I not been punished enough? How much more do I have to go through? I've had enough. I've had enough!"

After this release and more tears I began to calm down. I felt I needed to do that so that I could let go of something myself. That night I did some self healing for a long period of time. In the night a voice spoke to me, it was a female. She said "Remember where you came from." Then I was shown a baby. The scene went back in 3 stages. The first scene was of a beautiful new born baby. The second scene was in the 2nd trimester of pregnancy. The third scene was going back to a foetus. The whole of this vision was very real and clearly I was awake. What an amazing thing to see. It was all in full colour and felt as though the baby was me. Just as the female voice said 'remember where you came from' that had made me remember where I had come from.

We were born and brought into this world. The pattern here was telling me I had grown and developed. We came with innocence and would grow, learning our lessons. Was this the voice replying to what I had asked earlier that day? Was I to learn lessons in my life, the life that directed me? Was this my Karma, debt or credit? Have these challenges and difficulties been my lessons because of my positive and negative actions from previous lives?

Waking the next day I wondered if the dizziness was still with me. To my pleasant surprise I felt great, no dizziness just a relaxed and a feeling of well-being. Lying in bed I picked up Jean Kelford's book to read. This lady was one of the authors at the 'Second Sight' evening. I bought her signed copy and was fortunate to speak to her. I swiftly opened the book to a page titled 'Hairy Experiences', but I had no inclination why I was led to that page. As I lay comfortably I started to read and could not believe what it was all about. Jean explained in the book that we all have an animal guide to help us in our time of need. Jean had a silver back gorilla as her animal guide. Reading into her book I realised that the silver back gorilla I had been seeing around the house was looking after me! The gorilla was my protector, the one to give me courage and to be with me in my time of need. I could not wait to show Daren. He actually sat and listened. I was overjoyed at that point, glad that I was not seen to be imagining things. Somebody else had also sensed the presence of an animal and yet again a gorilla. What a relief that was for me. I felt very content that day, joy was within me.

After having an easy going day we watched television before retiring to bed.

My daughter had gone out for the New Year's Eve celebration with her friends. They could not book a taxi as there was none available. Daren was working early the next morning which left me to pick the girls up. I did not mind so much as I had rested in the day.

Seeing is Believing

I had said to Daren that I would wake up at 11.45pm to go and collect Sharon and her friends. I had fallen into a deep sleep for a couple of hours. Whilst asleep I heard a voice say "Wake up." It was a male voice. I looked at the clock and the time was 11.46pm. Amazed that I had received help to wake up in time, I thanked the voice. I just knew this was the voice of an angel. At 12.15am I struggled to ring or text as the airwaves were very busy. We needed to be in contact as we had not arranged the pick up point. Trying to contact tirelessly I became a little worried. Time was ticking away and obviously being a parent can be worrying at times. I decided to ask Jesus Christ for his help and I finally got in touch. She answered the phone and subsequently we made plans for the pick up. Looking at the digital clock just before putting the receiver down the time was 1.13am. It was the Ascended Masters number. The number to let me know, that the Masters were telling me to stay positive. Well everything was fine and I remembered to thank the help from the Great Ones.

Falling asleep I asked God to let me know what was going to happen next. I was then woken to be shown a scene in full colour of me emptying things into bags. With my eyes closed I saw a big domestic bin and I was getting rid of things in black bin liners. The message I was receiving was obvious, I was to have a clear out.

I had already had a sort out of unused items. But the message was stating I needed to do more of it.

Chapter Twelve

The Premonition

On the 2nd of January 2007, it was a dull, bitterly cold morning. I drove my niece to the bus station as she was returning home after spending a couple of days with us. As I walked a hundred yards or so to the area where the National Express Coach was to arrive I had a premonition. I saw the words 'National Express Coach Crash.' For a brief two seconds I saw the coach lying on its side. Blinking my eyes and puzzled as to what I saw I was quick to converse with my inner self. I said, "She's fine she is protected."

In deep thought I reminded myself that my niece was safe as she had received healing the day before and Archangel Michael had protected her. I then told myself to stop being silly.

Still astounded and lost in my own thoughts, my niece was speaking to me but I felt a million miles away. Her voice echoed and became louder as I was then aware of where I was walking. For that short time I was completely detached. When I had shrugged of the phenomenon we said our goodbyes to my niece and then she boarded the coach. I let go of the premonition and thought no more of it.

As it was the school holidays I did not meditate much. I had missed the daily ritual, it had become an essential part of my life, though I knew I could continue on a regular basis in just a few days time, when the children returned to school.

In the night I was shown some famous faces. I knew of some of them and there were some well-to-do people that I did not know the names of. After this vision I was shown red and gold flames. They were beautiful. The flames signified vitality and courage. This also intuitively told me to release any stress with my heart and soul's desire. At that moment I was not aware that I was stressed about my spiritual life path desires.

Seeing is Believing

Falling back asleep I dreamt of Robbie Williams and a sister with whom I did not have much contact. Well I suppose many of us would like to dream of the famous talented singer. It was a vivid dream. We were chatting and preparing food for a party. This was teaching me that we are all children of God and love is widespread. Rich or poor, black or white, we can all get along and live in harmony and joy.

Becoming disturbed from the wonderful dream of socialising with the rich and famous I was restless and woke up at 5am. I tossed and turned for a good couple of hours.

The television alarm came on at 7am. What appeared on the screen shocked me. As I sat up I could not believe it.

It was a news flash. In front of my eyes read, 'National Express Coach Crash.' In shock I tried to whisper to my husband as he sat up to watch this too.

I felt choked and flabbergasted. My heart was beating fast, I felt subdued. Staring at the screen we listened attentively. I managed to whisper to my husband again about my premonition. He somehow was unresponsive as I stared at him for a reply. After a while he murmured, 'Really.' I felt that he did not believe me. Then I carried on watching what the damage was to the lives of the people involved. There was loss of lives. My heart sank.

I did not know why I was shown the premonition. I did think it could be because I was psychic. I am not as psychic as some people and I am no medium. But why was this shown to me?

All day long I thought about what had happened. After a while I shared my thoughts with my family. I think some believed me and some did not.

After much contemplation the answer was obvious. I was made aware of the crash because I am a soul transferor. I was to help the souls move to the light. I was to send prayers and light to those who died and those suffering. As soon as I realised this I did my duty. I was left with some degree of sadness but some part of me told me it was their destiny. That was their life plan.

Guidance for My Future?

The following night, or should I say, at five o'clock in the morning, I was woken up with another message. I was shown my business shoe again, this time with a heart. The message revealed was to have the courage to go ahead with some kind of business or work.

I now began to think that I was to start something new, healing was what I enjoyed and wondered if this was what I was being encouraged and guided to do.

Shortly after, I was shown an old cottage door with a sparkling horseshoe. The lucky horseshoe on the door was very clear. It reminded me of an old countryside cottage.

Underneath the sparkly, lucky horseshoe were some words. The two words read 'no room.' Instantaneously I felt that it was saying there was no room at the inn. Why was I shown there was no room, no room for what? I felt disheartened. But not letting it upset me too much I fell back to sleep.

As the days led into January I began to feel different. I was more positive and knew that changes could be made and achieved.

I have always had challenges but I thought I could not cope with more of them. My soul felt it really had had enough, what else was I to endure? It would be easier to curl up and forget about where I really, truly wanted to be in life. But my motivation and determination would not let me, just as in the past.

Magically for me, I would soon overcome both my illness and my fears. I had the support of the angels and Ascended Masters. For those who do know there is something out there, but are not sure what, why not try communicating with the angels? I do feel there are a lot of people who would benefit from conversing with their own guardian angels, since we all have them. They may envelope you and you might feel their love as I do. They are there, waiting to help us, so ask for guidance and see what the response is.

Yet another night of guidance, I was again shown some numbers. There was a 3, 2, and then a 1 appeared in my closed eye view. The big bold numbers took me to a beautiful vision of a unicorn. The unicorn appeared in white light. Inside the unicorn outline I could see a mother and daughter. The scene was calming and beautiful. This was magical.

No, my mind was not playing tricks on me, it was not a myth. I can understand those sceptics who understand that a unicorn is a mythical animal illustrated in children's books but I do believe that there were once unicorns. Just like many of us see fairies and angels, some of us do see unicorns. However, I am unsure of their true significance.

After seeing the unicorn and the parent and child, there was also a star. Yes, the star was part of my name so I was sure that this message was referring to me.

Straight after being shown the star, a jet plane was taking off and then I heard fireworks.

As always I was prepared with a pen and paper to write down what I was shown. Notes were made after each important message was received.

In the early hours of the morning I asked the angels whether it was time for me to move on, as I was ready for changes. The response came back with an image of a book. The image then led to an enormous star in front of my closed eye view. As that faded I was given an image of thumbs up.

Well this was all telling me a great deal of information. The unicorn was, perhaps, telling me that I required spending more time with my children. That day I made more of a conscious effort to do so. The star related to me as my name means a cluster of stars, the jet taking off was telling me I was going to do well and the fireworks that there would be celebrations to come.

After asking the angels whether it was time for me to move on the answer was clear, they wanted me to write this book. I had their permission and it was good. Well, what could be more promising than that?

After waking up feeling so positive and knowing that I was ready to move on, I took the decision to take myself further both physically and spiritually. I wanted good health more than ever. I wanted to be of service and in the light. I wanted to be a lightworker.

All that time of having breathlessness, chronic fatigue and fibromyalgia, I had only wanted to recover. I wanted to go out to work and working with children was what I enjoyed doing.

Now I realise I had to be patient and all would be well. My life lessons needed to be learned and my life plan was in motion. My fate was to go through the pain, the helplessness, the inadequacy and suffering. God and I had already decided this was to be, before my birth.

All of my life I have wanted to help others, and believe this was my life purpose. Sometimes we do not stop and think who we are, where we came from and what our life purpose is.

I do believe and realise now that I have been approached many times in my life to be on the spiritual path. Just to confirm that, I have just received a message that, 'yes it is true, they have tried before to receive me on the spiritual path but I was not then ready.'

When I became ill again, I had time to reflect. I wondered why this was happening to me. Why, again and again, was I left in debilitating conditions? These were the times when I wondered what had I done so wrong that these situations were put upon me. As I have mentioned, I was supposed to stop and reflect. Then the angels appeared to comfort me, reassure and guide me. This time I was not escaping, even though it meant taking away my health and career. I can now joke about them trapping me into the spiritual path. Now, I would not have my life any other way!

Staying With Love

Just as there are angels and the heavenly realms there is also darkness. Where there is heaven there is hell. The Holy Bible speaks of darkness. There are many people who look to the dark side, even though they may do so in innocence. These are the people who really do need help and light shining on their souls.

As well as love there is also fear. It is Love that we need to remain with. With love everything will follow. Love has no boundaries, love can be everywhere, in everyone and love has no restrictions. Send love, feel love, and transmute fear into love. Hug someone. Hug your friend, neighbour or your family. The hugs transfers love from one to another. Wish peace and love to one another.

Even though I say love has no restrictions, we humans restrict that love. I have in the past restricted my love too, because of not having enough trust. Trust again, so that the love can flow.

I now send love through the airwaves, to people I love and to those I have had distances with. I know that much love is returned and I feel the happiest person alive.

Someone once said to me that they could not send love and would not even dream of it, to a person they are in conflict with. I was quite saddened to hear this as I know from my own experiences that in the physical world and spiritually that is not the way forward. How would the person ever settle and overcome the troubles with the other person? The mind would be troubled therefore encouraging ill health. The soul wants peace. Why battle with it? The battle then becomes with oneself. These unresolved issues then are carried into the next incarnation.

Many people have asked me how I bounce back. I always used to say 'You just keep going. Once one hurdle was over with you deal with the next one.'

All right so we do feel down and fed up now and again but let's appreciate what we have got. I have always told my children about

145

starving people all around the world and how they do not have decent clothes or even shelter.

We have roofs over our heads, food to eat, we can keep warm, and we have light. What about those in the poorer countries that do not have luxuries like us? The children who search for food in rubbish tips, no shelter, curled up feeling cold, they appreciate being alive. They have nothing, but I bet they have big hearts. So if they can bounce back and remain in life with so little, so can we.

Watching documentaries about the poor and hungry is unbearable, and yes, it makes my heart weep but I send those the prayers and universal love. A good friend once said to me we can do practical things too, like sharing our resources and our money. That is true, that is why we have numerous worthwhile and appreciated charities.

I am now grateful for my lessons in life, I have learned a lot and the challenges have made me stronger. I have a better understanding of the rules of life. I have no doubt there will be more challenges but coping with them should make my life easier through my spiritual understanding.

Following my gut instinct or intuition has been my guide too. One of my visions told me that I was opening up telepathically. Many of us have these experiences. If you think of your own life, I am sure this has happened to you at times. Telepathy is a natural human function. For me it was just that knowing. Knowing what someone was about to say and even telephoning someone at the precise moment that they had thought of me. Please do not misinterpret this, I am not claiming to be a genius, as I cannot read people's minds.

Seeing is Believing

Unafraid

My oracle cards were urging me to move forward fearlessly. But to what extent I did not know. Following my intuition and my strong urge to help, I did not fear.

Maybe I jumped two feet first into the swamp to save that unicorn I mentioned earlier, but I saw it as my duty. All will be revealed as to what happened here.

A child had been suffering for sometime with abnormal behaviour which the parents had become aware of. She was an eleven year old girl, obviously reaching puberty. The child had felt insecure for sometime. Insecurity led to an anxiety type illness. After receiving medical assurance of no serious diagnosis, the mother still worried frantically. Prior to meeting them it was already confirmed to me by the angels that there was no serious medical condition. After many tests, days later the lady told me nothing had been found by the doctors. After this conversation with the mother I was urged to help. The information that was coming through was that the child had allowed a negative entity into her broken aura. The entity was controlling her. The child could be helped if she wanted to be helped. Offering help to the family as I was guided to did not worry me. The mother accepted healing and the healing took place with the child's acceptance too. The frail child was desperate to be well so she could resume school. Feeling the hurt and emotions from her I really wanted to help. The child enjoyed the relaxing and calm feeling it gave her.

That very night I had a vision of a fork. The angels were telling me that the child needed tuning in. The child was out of balance in her mind, body and spirit. This was true since the mother had reported strange happenings with her daughter. A while later a vision of a television came through with a separate aerial. The angels were making sure I received the message.

Advice was given to take the child to a qualified, reputable healer in their locality as they lived at some distance from me. The healing helped the child and the parent was grateful. Although they had no knowledge of spiritualism they became aware of spiritual concepts. They began to notice changes with the help of the angelic beings. The child even dreamt of the angels as well as receiving messages.

I too had received a sign, it was a rose. This was a message from the angels signifying 'thanks with love.'

Although I realised that fear can attract fear, with some help from the young healer I understood this more fully.

The angels were there to guide me and they did look after me as they promised. It was remarkable to say the least. My daughter had dreams of the angels protecting the entire area surrounding the house. She told me they were everywhere and at every door. My son too had backed this up by his dreams. We had then in turn seen a boy of about thirteen years old wandering around in the house as well as outside. This boy was not in the physical world. He appeared to us for a reason. Alysha had told me his name was Michael. I instantly knew this was Archangel Michael. He was protecting me as I was dealing with negative energies. This confirmed even more the reality of being protected by Archangel Michael. It was really happening. Again I thanked the angels for all of their support. As I have mentioned before, my children are spiritual too but they have little idea of how much. I wish for them to continue to feel safe themselves, although at that time I did not need to tell them why Archangel Michael was present.

Sometimes though there are people who want spiritual help and then there are those who do not. It is an individual choice whether spiritual help is preferred by a person and respected if not. The soul of the person may not want to receive healing as they are not spiritually ready for it.

Seeing is Believing

Angelic Help

I had been praying for financial support to come our way over the last few weeks. Daren had wanted to sell his walking boots on a popular internet site. After finally making his preparations he asked me to do some final checks with his advert. He even asked me to ask the angels to help sell the boots. Instantly, I replied that he should ask himself. It was almost as if he did not believe in angelic existence but wanted to reap the rewards. I explained that he too did have a guardian angel and he would also benefit by conversing with them. But he was still not 100% convinced, as he had not experienced the angels himself. However I had supported him to some degree with his advert. Once the advert was widely sighted on the internet he kept a regular check on the progress.

After spending time with family across the miles, we returned to unpack and prepare the children for school the following morning. The telephone rang. It was my sceptical brother-in-law Paul, who informed us about Daren's boots for sale on the internet, he told us that the price had shot up remarkably high. Better still the company that had put the bid up were called Auction Angel! As Paul had become quite excited on the telephone with Daren, Daren in turn shouted to tell me of this wonderful news. I too became very excited. Before long everyone in the house was jumping up and down with joy. I do not think that Paul could quite believe this himself as he was the one who always disbelieved me. We immediately put everything on hold to check the information for ourselves. Amazingly there it was. Auction Angel had surpassed the price, making my wish for more money enter our home. Incredibly still, the price added up to a 9, which if divided by 3 gives us 3. Three is The Trinity to Divine Truth. For me there was sufficient evidence of Divine support. My heart was bursting with joy. Paul and Daren would now contemplate on the meaning of my beliefs. Thank You, God.

My angelic guidance cards were telling me to write a book as I do have leadership over it. I was also reminded to eat healthily and look after my overall well-being as this was important for my future. The guidance cards were also telling me everything was occurring as it should. I was at the right place in life.

The vision of the rose had reappeared to me during my sleep. I was then shown a square which indicated that I was now living for what I had not finished in a previous life.

Things were making sense to me as I have been approached by the celestial beings before but I was not then ready for the transformation. I sincerely believe that I was rescued and helped by the angels to fulfil my life purpose. There was no getting away from it now.

The Tour

That very same night, I was shown a beautiful golden swan. The golden shining sun also appeared before my closed eyes. Still awake I wondered where this would lead me.

Shortly afterwards, I was taken to a beautiful interior of someone's house, it had luxurious furniture. The natural pale wooden floor complimented the cream leather sofas. Out of one room, and then entering the dining room there was a beautiful dining table with cushioned chairs. In the centre of the table there were fresh flowers in a vase. The house was immaculate. The tour led into the kitchen. This area was shown very briefly but from what I can remember of it, it too was in pristine condition. I was later led to the exterior of the building. It was a fantastic structure with a double garage. The drive was big enough to fit about six cars on. After some time I wondered why I was shown this view. As I thought, instantly I was shown a journey maybe by car. It was a journey through a village, with little cottages on either side of me. The journey then took me along a narrow lane; there were fields

150

surrounding the lane. Returning to the drive just as I saw earlier, the house stood grand before my sight again. Another tour of this dwelling took me around the living room and briefly the dining room again I had now become quite excited. My heart was warm with excitement. Could this be my future home? Well I suppose I could dream.

The same vision appeared to me for a couple of days. The swan was telling me to trust the grace of both the physical and spiritual planes and their gifts. The sun related to healing energy for my self and to banish any depressed state on any level. Although I can quite honestly say I felt very content. The vision of the house was maybe trying to tell me that I could achieve something grand.

Be Careful

After days of ease and no rushing of the world around me, we decided to spend a few hours out and about. Alysha, Daren and I made plans to go to a town nearby, in particular to a bookshop and for lunch. Daren, a keen reader was always buying books. As he was driving towards the town, I briefly closed my eyes and I received a message. The message was scribed before my eyes. It clearly read, 'Be careful.' I knew it came as a warning. But not sure when this message was for, I thanked the angels as usual. I never took the messages for granted as they were my guidance. They were a privilege to receive.

Daren parked the car then we crossed the road into the shopping precinct. Daren decided he wanted to visit a few other shops too whilst in the area. So we planned to go our separate ways and to meet in a short while. Not long after setting off my energies were becoming depleted. I watched people walk past me, realising I was losing my strength rapidly. I needed a sit down very quickly. Alysha and I looked for a coffee shop nearby. We found one not too far away. Luckily the busy coffee shop had one last small table vacant. As I sat and reached for my crystals in my bag I was aware of needing a boost of energy. Holding my clear quartz and amethyst crystal I prayed for help with my fatigue.

I closed my eyes for a brief minute. Alysha understood what I was doing by now as she had seen me in this state many times. I had to sit and rest whilst my energies returned. The lunch that I ordered had arrived and I was only too ready for any extra nutrients that could replenish me. Shortly afterwards we made contact with Daren who then joined us. I explained what had happened. My message was telling me to be careful of draining my energies. Bizarrely, a thought had come to my mind as I was becoming fatigued. The people I was passing were draining me. They were spiritually sucking away my energies. Initially I felt well enough to make the short trip into the precinct, it was making sense. However, I felt a little better before we left the coffee shop.

Free the Spirit

After the angels had shown me that I needed to have a clear out a couple of weeks earlier, I made my decision to do just that. This was now a different sort of clear out. Everything I had built up over the last five years was to go. My intuition was telling me I had to clear everything. It was to be a new start. The start would be to sell my business items to gain the money for this book. As the decision was now final I made the necessary contacts. At that time I was extremely positive and I knew it was the correct decision. Telling my friends and family was exciting for me but they were somewhat concerned as to whether it was the correct decision. There was no proof of anything for them. To be truthful there was no tangible proof for me either. I had to have blind faith that things would work out. I was making room for the new. 'Out with the old and in with the new.' This was the way I needed to view this situation. The visions and my own intuition were enough to spur me on. After all the preparations of selling all that I owned were good. The days approached and my living room looked like Aladdin's cave, people arrived to select what they wanted. Initially I was excited, but then grief set in. It was not grief of losing a person but a grief of loss of my identity almost. The cultural work I did was part of my life. It was heart wrenching. I could not believe that it could have been so painful. Feeling deep sadness I sat in contemplation. Then in my view came Saint Germain and Djwal Khul the Ascended Masters of transformation and healing. They looked at me questioning why I had become so sad and fearful. I apologised for any mistakes I had made and told them I would now sort myself out. As I was feeling a little more confident, I then reassured myself that things would be fine. It was just a materialistic letting go. During this day I had also seen my Gorilla in the mist. He appeared to me whilst I was meditating. He had a sad face once again. I was reassured he would help me and I felt happy to see him. Some time ago I heard a male voice in the middle of the night. It was not Daren's voice; it said the word 'Onch,' and I wondered was this his name?

During the night I was woken to be shown Mickey Mouse. It was great to see this. Mickey was sitting on a rock in the middle of a lake. It was beautiful and in full colour. But he sat with his knees close to his face and his arms resting on his knees. He was sad. After indulging in this beautiful view for a brief few minutes, I was then shown him swimming to shore. This message was clear. They wanted me to pull myself out of the sad situation. Also during the night another message came through, it was that 'wisdom and healing have the speed to change but without the fear.' After being shown the polar bear I knew the message was to 'remain grounded and to have no fear of power on the physical plane.'

One day I woke to find a message from spirit warriors. This may well only have looked like a smudging but the shape of a man standing sideways was visible. Above he was releasing a bird which looked like a dove. It appeared clearly to me as a Native American spiritual man setting a bird free. This message too spoke clearly to me. I was told 'set the spirit free.'

Image of free the spirit

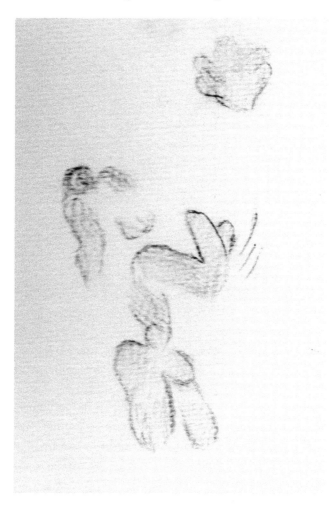

The communication was coming imminently thick and fast from the Ascended Masters and spirit animals I was being told that I travelled between 'Physical and Spiritual' realms. This was true as I had often said to Lyn that I was sure that in the night I was not in my physical body. I sometimes landed with such a bump that I woke up feeling breathless. It almost felt like I had been very busy working whilst sleeping. I know that some of you readers will be now questioning is this why I suffer with breathlessness? Well I can almost agree with that. I am now not as drained by other people's energies as I have become stronger. My life is more positive through my personal healing journey.

As the days of clearing my unused items were progressing, I was shown my business shoe, a bird flying and a book with a face of a Buddha.

Now my understanding of this was that I would be in business, it will be fine, it could be achieved as well as writing a book; it will be a spiritual book.

Which leads me on to saying that this is where I am now, the book is now complete. However the visions are still appearing and the guidance is still coming. With thanks to the Angels and Ascended Masters.

After word

My spiritual Journey has transformed my life for the better. I am a simple person, who likes simplicity. With passion and dedication I am here to help serve The Divine. My life purpose is clear as I am here to spread the light, to free souls that are trapped and give direction to lost souls. My hunches, intuitions, The Masters and The Angels have guided me to where I am today.

Coincidences? Well everything that has happened in the six months that is written about in this book I can honestly say were not coincidences. They are what are known as synchronicities.

Healing has helped many people who have experienced it. I am sure many more will try Angelic Reiki. You do not have to have a religious belief for the healing to work. It is what God wants us to have. It is a gift. Receive it and thank those whom give it to you as they are the channel for this beautiful gift. Those receiving Angelic Reiki are connecting with pure Divine energies. Receive the healing and be thankful for it.

✿ ✿ ✿

- The animal spirits come to give us messages and guidance.
- Thank nature for the beauty we have around us and appreciate it.
- The souls that pass over, send them love and be assured they are in the right place.
- Spend time in the moonlight, under the stars and in the warmth of the sun.
- Take time-out meditating, refresh the soul.
- Eat healthily, sleep well and exercise when you can.
- Look after your mind, body and spirit.

The summary of this book is that, having no strong religious background and no particular prophet or spiritual master to believe in, I am constantly awed by the spiritual nature of the world around me and life itself. I have always connected with Jesus Christ but not aware of how much until recently. The angels are very new in my life, although I still believe that they have approached me in my adulthood. How would anyone ever believe me is what I have wondered whilst on my spiritual journey since 2006. Yet with the guidance from above I now have this book complete. I knew I could not keep my experiences quiet! Those who know me will say I never stop talking, so perhaps this is why I am used as a voice. I have profound belief in Angels, The Ascended Masters and The Divine. I feel I have happiness and fulfilment in my life. Therefore I wish that you have happiness and fulfilment in your life too.

Look out for the next book!

I cannot make any health claims regarding the alternative therapies that I have discussed in this book. What I can say is that many people have found the benefits from the therapies that I offer.

Simple Meditation

- Sit or lie down
- Make yourself comfortable
- If sitting place both feet flat on the ground
- Close your eyes
- Take in three deep breaths (as far as you feel comfortable)
- Let go of stress and tensions of the day
- Allow your body to relax
- Stay in the calm for 5 minutes
- Take in three breaths
- Bringing your awareness back to the room
- Feel your feet touching the ground
- Open your eyes
- Wiggle your toes and fingers

Recommended Reads

An Angel Saved My Life
Jackie Newcomb

Embracing Love
Liz Adamson

Is it you! Or is it spirit?
Jean Kelford

A Little Light on the Spiritual Laws
Diana Cooper

Angel Medicine
Doreen Virtue

Angel Numbers
Doreen Virtue
Lynette Brown

Earth Angel
Doreen Virtue

Archangel oracle cards
Doreen Virtue

Healing with the Fairies Oracle Cards
Doreen Virtue

Magical Mermaids and Dolphins
Doreen virtue

The stories in this book are accounts of real life experiences. They are written with utmost, heartfelt honesty by a simple person wanting simplicity.

Coincidences? Well everything that has happened in the last six months of Parveen's life, is in this book. She believes they were not coincidences but rather synchronicities. Events that led from one place to another, and the chance meetings with those people who have now become special in her life.

Even her healing abilities were not coincidental. Each has been a synchronistic event.

The visions were guidance from the Angels and God and it was all happening for a reason. The reason was for transformation.

For those of you whose eyes are closed, open them and awaken your soul.

Parveen holds Angel Evenings on a monthly basis. The workshops are enlightening for those whom are awakening to spirituality.

Parveen is also a Master Teacher in Angelic Reiki.

To contact Parveen email: parveen.angels@yahoo.co.uk
For more information: www.clusterofstars-angels.co.uk